MARINE MYSTIQUE

To Chad I hope you enjoy the reading, Old boys Boot Kamp I wish you success in all your future Endeavors. Keep your powder dry and stay safe

Fred Henary
Semper Fi

MARINE MYSTIQUE

Frank Hernandez

To order additional copies of this book, contact:
Xlibris Corporation
1-888-7-XLIBRIS
www.Xlibris.com
Orders@Xlibris.com

CONTENTS

To the loving memory of my Son, Frank Jr. He was never a Marine, but had the ability to put up with this Marine's Bull, Always, Always, with his special smile.

"*I have grown to look upon Marines as something sacred. I have laughed with them . . .cried, cursed, suffered, fought and bled with them . . . I have buried them. And all the time, I have loved them.*"

Author Unknown

PROLOGUE

It's hard to believe that nearly thirty years have gone past since my graduation from the Marine Corps School for Drill Instructors, (D.I.s) at Marine Corps Recruit Depot, (MCRD), San Diego, California, and ten years since my retirement from the United States Marine Corps.

I recently had the opportunity to visit MCRD, and memories of my D.I. days came flooding back. Much has changed over the last thirty years. More importantly, much has remained the same. The SingSong cadence of the D.I.'s, as they herded their charges from one location to another. The ever present sound of "Sir, Yes Sir!" as the recruits responded to the commands of their D.I.'s., and the sounds of Aircraft arriving and leaving the Airport located adjacent to the Depot.

Marine! the name is synonymous with all that is held high in soldierly virtue. What is it? that changes a group of young men who come from all parts of the country with different racial, social, economic, religious and political backgrounds, into a brotherhood of men, with a bond so great they are willing to die for one another.

I believe it is the common shared experience of recruit training, where they are first introduced to the history, pride, traditions of the United States Marine Corps. It is a tradition that they can only become part of, after proving themselves worthy of the title Marine. This introduction is done by the D.I.'s and subsequently reinforced by their fellow Marines, with the added knowledge that once recruit training is completed you are now a member of the finest fighting outfit in the world. Once a Marine, always a Marine. With a kinship and a mystique that will follow you for the rest of your life.

Anytime I attended any type of social function, be it a picnic, dinner or just a couple of cold ones with friends, the conversation always seem to lead to my Marine days and ultimately to my tenure as a Drill Instructor. What was it like to be a D.I.? Those asking the questions always seemed to enjoy my stories, so I thought, "What the hell", why not put them on paper!

Some readers my find some terms used in the book foreign to them, specifically the rank structure. One enters the enlisted world of the Marine Corps as a Private or E-1 the latter is considered to be a pay grade. There are nine enlisted pay-grades, for example a Sgt is a (E-5) and a SgtMaj/MGySgt a (E-9). You should never ever refer to a Marine in terms of a pay-grade, only by rank. Conversely, the Warrant Officer and Commissioned Officers are also in categories of rank and pay grade. Warrant Officer (W-1) to Chief Warrant Officer Five (CWO-5) and Commissioned Officers, Second Lieutenant (0-1) to Four Star General (0-10).

THE BEGINING

This night was typical of a Southern California summer evening, specifically one at the Marine Corps Recruit Depot, San Diego California. It was a night that could have been really warm except for the ocean breeze circulating throughout the depot. I had just stepped out of our company office, officially known as Lima Company, 3rd Recruit Training Battalion, for a quick smoke. The company office is an old World War II vintage style Quonset hut, as are the majority of the buildings on the recruit depot. I tasted the acrid smoke of my cigarette, and listened to the overwhelming sounds of the aircraft arriving and leaving San Diego's International Airport. " Pain in the ass" if you ask me, I thought, and one helluva a place to train recruits, those damn airplanes always drowning out the sound of your voice everytime you gave commands to the recruits. Oh well, Semper Fi Mac!

"Hey Hernandez! Get your Mex Ass in here", shouted Sgt. Taglieri, hearing my name brought me back to reality. I entered the company office and scanned the room, we were all present, my fellow D.I.s and myself. We gathered round the Gunny's desk waiting for the word that would start us on our way to another training cycle of more than 13 weeks during which we were supposed to transform civilians into United States Marines.

The year is 1970 and the Viet Nam War rages on, The Gunny has split us into teams of D.I.'s each team consisting of at least three members, two drill instructors and the team leader or Platoon Commander (Plt. Cmdr.). His status is signified by his broad and very highly polished black belt. We D.I.'s would wear the standard issued cartridge belt and all of us topped our uniforms with the coveted Campaign Cover (Hat), commonly called Smokies.

Drill instructors or range personnel only wore this cover, but the latter did not count in our estimation. You see, we believed that only those Marines training recruits and having earned the honor by graduating from the Marine Corps School for D.I.'s should be allowed to wear these smokies. We even referred to ourselves as Hats and we felt we were the best the Corps had to offer. We were all Non-Commissioned Officers and our particular group were all Viet Nam veterans. "Listen up" commands the Gunny, "We have a series waiting for pickup at receiving barracks. I want the same routine we always have for any new series." A series is a group of platoons consisting of 80 to100 men. " I want all of you to go to receiving to pickup the platoons. This is the breakdown, 1st Plt goes to Navarre, 2nd to Yordt, 3rd to Bosch and the 4th to Mimiaga. When you get there I want those goats (recruits) herded back to our area with a seabag drag and the fear of God placed into them before you bed them down for the night. Questions?" "I hope these turds are better than the last batch," I said to no one in particular.

So starts the ritual of transformation of over 300 men into a United States Marine. The 4 platoons would be part of a series, headed by a Series Officer (First Lieutenant, (0-2)), Series Gunnery Sergeant (E-7) and the Plt Cmdrs with their teams of D.I.'s. We were all members of a Battalion that belong to a Regiment forming a perfectly structured table of organization. We had all worked together in past platoons, and I had to admit we formed one helluva a group. We all had different personalities and different backgrounds but all of us had one thing in common, a love for our Corps, and our pledge to ensure only those young men qualified would become United States Marines. Our team would consist of Staff Sergeant (E-6), Navarre the Plt Cmdr., Sgt. Morse and myself, both of us were buck Sergeants (E-5) and would serve as his junior D.I.'s. In our series the Plt Cmdrs were referred to as Boss by the junior D.I.'s. Hey Boss! "Whats our plan of attack" asked Morse. Ssgt Navarre who stands about 5 feet 6 inches was a wiry mean Son of a Bitch, and was fast approaching his third year on the Drill Field, replied "I want those goats placed in a constant state of terror from the moment they see you two. Then we will have my usual introduction." We both knew what he meant by his usual introduction, because this would be our third platoon as a team. We knew what the Boss wanted and more importantly what it was he expected. "Well let's do it! He roared." And so the training of men into Marines was about to begin.

We walked from the Company Office to the receiving area, a distance of about one-mile I could not help wondering how many other Hats had made this same journey to meet their new charges. For the next 13 weeks the young men we were about to meet would for all practical purposes, belong to us. Ironically our route took us past the Recruit Depot's theater, where 13 weeks from today a command of "Dismissed" would be given to our platoon, and for the first time, they would be referred to as Marines. Until that day we would do our best to ensure that they would become worthy of that title.

As we approached the receiving area we could see a group of men wearing yellow sweatshirts, utility trousers and white tennis shoes, all wearing their utility covers (hats) atop freshly cut hair. Hair my ass, they were now completely bald, wiping away all remnants of their past civilian life. They were now standing outside the barber shop, seabags in hand, each standing on a set of yellow footprints that had been painted on the pavement in a perfect copy of a platoon in formation. The seabags contained their basic issue of clothing, toilet articles etc . . .Upon leaving the barbershop they had been given instructions to stand on the yellow footprints, and not move or talk as they waited for the arrival of their D.I.'s. They had probably been waiting less than thirty minutes, and since they still were basically nothing more than bald civilians, were not doing anything they were told. They had been on the recruit depot for less than a week taking tests, physicals and just miscellaneous bullshit. We just considered this a week of enjoyment at the taxpayers expense. All this time they were being led around by a troop handler or escort to show them were things were located, and to take them from one place to another. They, of course had seen D.I.s as they went through this introduction phase but had not yet been assigned to their Battalion, Series, or Platoon, at least not till we showed up. We could see them talking and just having a good old time. This lark was about to come to a screeching halt. They say ignorance is bliss!

"Who the Fuck told you to Move and Talk?" Morses voice boomed out of the darkness. "I fucking said who told you maggots to move?" He continued to yell at the top of his lungs, as he stormed into the group on the yellow footprints. He and I went from one recruit to the other, yelling and berating each one we approached. We continued up and down the line of men. "You think this is some damn civilian picnic?" Is that what you all think? When I ask a GodDamn question I expect a response from you assholes! Do you think this is some kind of picnic? You had all better reply and the first words out of those scummy mouths had better be Sir, once again sweeties, do you think this is some kind of picnic? "Sir No Sir," was now heard from the platoon. "Sgt Hernandez did you hear anything? One more time ladies and answer like you have a set of balls between those legs. Let me hear you sweeties! "Sir No Sir". Now there was complete silence, and not a muscle moved among the recruits, least the wrath of these two crazy men in smokies is brought back down on them.

Sgt Morse and I now marched to the front of the group, perfectly centered. We halted and then in unison faced the group. We knew that every eye would be upon us. "O K maggots," began Morse, "My name is Drill Instructor Sgt. Morse, I am not your mother, father, sister or brother nor your girlfriend because you won't repeat won't ever screw me. I am one of two of your Drill Instructors, and I am here to train your worthless bodies for the next 13 weeks. You had better now give your souls to God because your asses are now mine, do you understand me ladies?" No Response. "I said is that understood?" "Sir Yes Sir!" shouted 80 voices in response. "To my right is Drill Instructor Sgt. Hernandez, "Now it was my turn to speak" As you have just heard. Unless that civilian shit is still in your ears, we are here to train you and we will not cut any of you any slack in the training, do as you are told, when you are told and we will all get along just fine. Now I must admit you are the sorriest bunch of turds it has been my misfortune to look at, but sweeties that will fucking change! Now shitheads I want you to turn around, Not Yet! That means you shit-for-brains, in this Marine Corps we do everything as a team, Do You Understand!? "Sir yes Sir!" I can't hear you! "Sir yes Sir" they all shouted. "Now when I give you the word you will turn around. Do It!"

They were all now looking a the Marine Corps version of a trash container or Dippsty Dumpster, Immediately the top lids flew open and then, as if shot from a cannon the Plt Cmdr, Ssgt Navarre, leapt out among the recruits. Like a cat, Navarre lands on his feet, and then goes to the front of the Plt. He lets the effects of his entrance sink in before he starts to speak. Unlike Morse and myself, Navarre does not yell but speaks in a soft yet quite audible voice. "I am your Plt Cmdr, Ssgt Navarre, I wear this black belt that symbolizes my status as the Plt Cmdr. I have been a Drill Instructor and God help you scum if I ever take this belt off and replace it with the cartridge belts of your D.I.s. Welcome to Marine Corps Recruit Depot, San Diego Ca."

"If you thought this was going to be a Boy Scout camp, I can tell you that you are just plain wrong. What you are attempting to do is join our club, the United States Marine Corps. The best military fighting force in the entire fucking world. Our symbol is the Eagle, Globe and Anchor. Many men have worn this symbol, but only after earning the right to wear it. And many good men have died while wearing it. Now I don't give a rats ass what any of you shitheads did before you got here. I don't care if you were captain of the football team or you graduated Magna Cum a lot, if your old man has money or if you were dirt poor. You see sweethearts, as of this moment you are about to be reborn, and have the opportunity to do as well as anyone else. But of course if you are as useless as you appear, the only thing I have to worry about is how much a bus ticket will cost the government to send your sorry butt back to your mama. We will be fair, at times you might even think cruel, but remember, our club is the most elite club in the world. You must and I will see to it that you are worthy to bear the title of United States Marine."

"Sgt's Morse and Hernandez will take you to our Company area, you're new home and bed you down for the night. Ok maggots, when I tell you, you will face to the left. Do It! Your other left you silly shit! When I say go you will start off with your left foot and continue to march. Ready go! "Our herd begins its journey into the martial world of Marine Boot Camp.

We would take the longest possible way back to the company area. Each recruit carried his seabag, we continued our verbal insults, Left, Right, Left was our marching cadence. "What the hell's wrong with you turds? When I say left your left foot strikes the deck, or the ground as you called it in civilian life. Oh shit stop, stop, stop! Let's just start all over again. Ready go! You there, with the big ears like a damn radar site, your other left foot! Do you know your left from your right? What the Fuck you mean you aren't sure? Here now, (stomping on his toes), the one that hurts is your left foot. Understand? "Ok Hippity Hop Mob Stop!"

It was now about midnight and we were finally at the company area. "Ok maggots we will now put you to beddy bye. This is now home for you." Pointing to the makeshift platoon, I now designated squads. "This group is the 1st squad, second, third, and fourth. When I give you the word you will very quickly go into the Quonset hut that is for your squad, you will take your seabags and open it up, take your linen out." "Sir what's linen?" came a voice out of the darkness. "What the hell you mean What's linen? Linen, for all you dumb fucks, is your sheets and blankets. What's Linen? Where in the hell did you maggots come from? Now once again, you will take your linen out, place it on your racks or beds, take your trousers off and your shoes, replace your shoes with the shower shoes in your seabag. Inside you will find footlockers, place all your shit inside the footlocker, and then stand in front of your racks. Those sleeping on the upper rack will stand on the left, those sleeping on the lower rack will stand on the right as you face the middle of your hut. We call that Inboard. Do you Understand? I can't hear You! Do You Understand!? You are now officially Plt 3009 . Plt 3009, Repeat it you shitheads! "Sir Plt 3009!" "Get into the Huts, Go! Go! Go."

Like a flushed covey of quail they rushed into their respective huts. We now went into our own hut, which was dully called the Duty Hut. Our hut was identical to the ones the recruits were now in, the only difference was that this would be not only our sleeping quarters, but also our office and was shared by the other Hats in the series. Consequently we had four field desks, about ten wall lockers for our uniforms and personal items and four racks. You see, 24 hours of each and every day these recruits would be under the supervision of a D. I. We put them to bed and we would be the ones waking them up. Every third night a member of the team spent the night with his charges on his duty day.

As the boss entered the duty hut Morse and I were seated around our field desk. He took his campaign cover off and as usual went and poured himself a cup of coffee. "Ok, you two have been around long enough to know the routine. Take them to the head, let them piss, then put them to sleep. I have the Duty tonight but Hernandez, I want you here at reveille, so you can wake them up and take care of our administrative shit. T-1 (training day) starts on Monday. That only gives us two days to flesh them out and get all the crap done that was not taught at D.I. School."

The yelling and screaming of the other members of our series could now be heard as they brought their recruits to the company area. They would be doing the same thing that we had been doing. "OK Morse you can shove off. Hernandez after you take them to the head and bed them down then you can take off. Hey Morse, since I have the duty, what are you going to do?" "Shit, its only 1230 I still have time to get the Anchor and shoot a couple of games of pool."

The Anchor was a little bar, just outside the front gate of the Recruit Depot, and was frequented by mainly off duty Hats. Morse knew that even if he did not have the duty, he was expected to come in to work anyway. But at least he could come in about 0900 (9AM). Our duty days were rotated, and would continue to be this way until the recruits graduated from Boot Camp. What was suppose to happen was that every third day we would have off, but we knew that for at least the first month and a half, the three of us would probably work each day, getting only the evenings off.

"Reveille, Reveille!" I screamed as I went from one Quonset Hut to the other. It was now 0500 (5AM) and I had only been gone for about 4 hours. "Reveille!" I shouted as I banged the lid of a trash can. I went into each Hut and woke the sleeping beauties, tossing over racks, yelling for them to get up. "Its time to wake up sweeties; you turds think you can sleep all day?" Entering the last hut, I was overwhelmed with the odor of urine. "What the Fuck?" "Which one of you shitheads, wet the bed? Speak Up, because if I have to find the rack then the recruit that peed his rack, he will have hell to pay." "Sir, I did" "I my ass, what the hell is wrong with you?" You always pee in the rack?" Now listen to me you turd, you will take your wet sheets and wrap them around your skuzzy body, Do it! Now you will put your left arm out and shape it like a spout, place your right hand on your hip. You now have a spout and a handle, except the real spout is between your legs. You will until I call the platoon to formation say the following, "I am a little pee pot, short and stout this is my handle and this and you will point to the real spout, is my spout." Understand! "Sir, yes Sir" "Do it!" "I am a little pee pot short and stout . . ." "Louder, I can't hear you."

It was not unusual to have a bed wetter, normally this would stop by just the sheer embarrassment and our having the Fire Watch wake their asses up every two hours to make a head call. If this did not solve the problem then we would have to send them to see the Doctor at sick call. If the recruit continued to have a problem then he would be discharged from the Corps.

Leaving the hut I went to the middle of the platoon area and continued to yell, this isn't the damn Army this is another wonderful and glorious day in the United States Marine Corps. Platoon 3009! Damn it, I said Platoon 3009 and I better hear every one of you Repeat what I said!" "Plt 3009!" "Sir Plt 3009!" "When I give you the word you will all get out of those huts and form a Plt formation on the Plt Street. Plt 3009 , Plt Formation , Do it!" "Bodies started to file out of the huts." "Move ! Move!" They were now formed on the street. "When in Plt formation you don't move, breathe, fart unless I tell you; is that understood? I cant hear you sweeties is that understood! Sir Yes Sir!. "OK sweeties we will now go to the Head (bathroom) so that you can pee. Face Left, Ready Go! Goddamn it! you start out with your left foot, Left, Right , Left . . .Plt Halt!"

"Now when I give you the word we will go into the head by squads, then rotate the squads in and out of the head. Then I will tell you to clear the Head and you had best get your tired asses out! Understood?" "Sir Yes Sir!" "Ok 1st squad into the Head, You have three minutes to do your business. Take your piss and get ready to get out!" Three minutes elapsed and now it was "Clear the Head!" "Sir Clear the Head" "Damn it I said to clear the head!" One individual was sitting on the pot as I walked into the Head. "Who the hell told you to take a shit, Piss means to Pee!" Oh I know, you are probably used to the word urinate. Now get the hell out of here! I don't care if you aren't finished, pinch off that turd and Move! Move! "The recruit leapt from the pot, trousers down around his ankles and attempted to run out and join his squad. Having marched back to the company we were back on the Plt. Street. "OK people, we will go back into our huts, get dressed in the same uniform that we found your sorry asses in. Once dressed you will fall back on the street in Plt Formation and we will be ready to go to morning chow. Is that Understood!? "I cant hear you; "Sir Yes Sir!" "Ready! Go, Go, Go! . . ."

We were now in a rush to cover all aspects of Marine Corps Life and every second of every minute had to be an opportunity to instruct these young men. We did not let any time go by as wasted time. With the Plt in formation I now spoke to them. "Up until now in order to get your worthless bodies moving you had been told to Go, Get, or whatever? When we start to march you will

-HERN

now hear the command of Forward March! Forward is what we call the preparatory command and March is the command of execution. This means that first we tell you what you will be doing, gives your head a chance to tell your ass then your feet, what it is you are going to do. Preparatory, Understand? Then we tell you to do it (Execution). Then, of course, you fucking do it! Understood? You will, upon hearing the command of execution, step forward with your left foot taking a full 30 inch step, 30 inches is measured from the heel of your right foot to the heel of the left. You will continue to take 30-inch steps, alternating between your left and right foot at our cadence. You will swing your arms naturally six inches to the front and three inches to the rear. Until you get your shit together, as a reminder you will sound off, upon hearing the preparatory command "Full 30 inch step Sir" Understood? "I will now demonstrate how the command will sound and then demonstrate the movement." I then demonstrated both the command and the movement for the recruits.

"OK, we will try it, but first we will do everything by the numbers. I will sound off the preparatory command Forward, you will say, A full 30-inch step Sir, I will then give the command of execution at which point you will step off. OK, face to the right Forward! March! Left right, left. Damn, I said swing your arms naturally not like a robot! While marching we must maintain 40 inches from the person in front of us. We must also maintain our alignment with the person to our right. Understood!? Left, Right, Left. I said 40 inches, you shithead, watch your alignment, Left, Right, Left." The sing song cadence continued as the recruits marched. At the same time we continued to remind them of alignment, swinging their arms, and the distance from one recruit to another.

"Hippity Hop Mob stop! This is our Mess Hall, When you enter the hatch, what your mommies called a door. You will take your covers off with your left hand, slap it on your left thigh and then enter the Mess Hall. We never ever wear our covers indoors unless we are armed, that is wearing a cartridge belt like mine or physically armed with a weapon, Understood? Once you have entered the Mess Hall you will take a mess tray and then sidestep through the chow line, take all that you want but you best eat all you take. You will not talk, you will then move to the tables provided. Place your trays on the table and wait till you are told to be seated. Once commanded to seat, you will eat and then get the Fuck out. A platoon formation will be formed outside the Mess Hall, you will fall in at the position of attention and god Help you if you screw around." As you would with children, we had to explain each and every thing a recruit was to do, not because they were as stupid as they seemed, but this was a whole new environment for them and the Corps emphasized that we do everything together. We knew that if we forgot the slightest item that this could affect the entire platoon. The recruits now went through the chow line as instructed. The slightest infraction bringing instant correction. "Hey numb nuts I told you to stand until you were told to be seated! The tables filled with the privates. "Ok Ready! Seat! No! No!, Get up, you will learn to move like one person, will try it again sweeties, Ready! Seat, Bullshit get back, Ready! Seat! OK, Eat!" No where and no place were the recruits free from correction. I continued to hear the other D.I. 's dressing down their charges. Sgt. Tagleri, was yelling at one of his charges; "Hey Sgt Hernandez this maggot doesn't seem to enjoy scrambled eggs." Now we had an unwritten rule that you never screwed around with another D.I.'s recruit unless the violation was such that it could not possibly be ignored. But if a Hat invited you to comment on what was happening then all bets were off. Tag continued; "Look at this turd's tray, he didn't eat half of what he took. What's the matter private were the eggs not cooked to your liking?" Several other D.I.s now joined us from our series. Each taking a turn at the recruit. "Maybe we should have the cook fix them sunny side up or maybe Eggs Benedict, like mommy you used to fix them for you, right! Private!? I know, its just too early in the morning for breakfast, huh, Mommy would probably bring them to you in bed. I am so sorry they are not to your liking, but I'll tell you what let's save them for later. Take all the shit you left on the tray and place them in your pockets so you can munch on them later. Oh yes, let's not forget the milk. "The entire contents of the tray to include the milk were now in the recruits pockets, including a banana which was sticking out the front of his top left pocket. "Now sweetie, you have a snack for later. You will from now on always eat what you take, right? "Sir Yes Sir." We knew that this action would surely stop future violations of recruits not eating all their chow. "Now says Tag, since you have thoroughly embarrassed me in front of my fellow D.I.s I suggest you and (screaming at the top of his lungs) Get The Fuck Out of my Sight, you scum bag!

All the members of my platoon had finished their meal and were now standing in platoon formation as they had been instructed. But even after all the bullshit they had been through since the day before, some of them still insisted on looking around and talking. "I don't believe you maggots. I leave you alone for just 3 minutes and you go back to that undisciplined civilian bullshit. I told you that you don't move, talk, look around when at the position of attention. Just wait until we get back to the company area. We will take care, of your sorry asses. Face to the Right, Forward March! Left, Right, Left!"

I marched the platoon back to the area; "Soo . . .you ladies think that when we are not looking you can just do what you want, and ignore any of the instructions that were given to you. Maybe a little exercise will help take that energy from your worthless bodies. OK, ladies you see the sandy area in front of our Huts? I said do you see the sandy area in front of my Huts? "Sir Yes Sir!" Well that area is our grass, but we also call it the pits. Now my undisciplined friends, get into the pits. I said Move! "The recruits scrambled into the pits standing wondering what was to happen next." "OK, get down in the pushup position, when I say one you will go down, two you will come up. You will repeat my count. Ready one!" "One Sir!" Now taking my time I would call out two, making the recruits struggle in each position. "One!" "One Sir!" "So you want to screw around do you?" "Sir No Sir!" "I can't hear you!" The pits were to become another dreaded but very familiar area to them. They would soon learn that infractions would cause instant correction, and that much of this correction was through the use of physical exercise and this took place in the pits.

After about ten minutes of this pushup drill I ordered the recruits back into the Quonset huts to prepare for the days training. "Get on your feet!" When I tell you, you will go inside your huts and grab your footlockers, place them on the Platoon Street, 1st, 2nd squad here, and 3rd and 4th squad here pointing to the designated area. You will place them so the rear of them is facing the Platoon Street. Understand? "Sir Yes Sir!" "Plt 3009, in the Huts!". I now stepped into the duty hut and seated at our field desk was the Boss, Ssgt Navarre. "OK Boss! the platoon is getting ready to place lockers on the street, they wanted to screw around after chow, so I introduced them to the pits." "Good," replied the boss, sipping his usual cup of coffee. "We will being doing the same shit as with every herd. Our next two days are Admin, with Monday starting T-1 (Training Day 1)."

As we spoke the sounds of the other Hats in the duty hut could also be heard. This would be an everyday occurrence. Some had recruits in the duty hut, explaining, yelling the corrections to infractions they had made the mistake of doing in view of their D.I.'s. Other Hats were yelling for the sheer joy of making noise, we knew the effect of our yelling on any and all recruits outside the Duty Hut. Most of our yells, were phrases of endearment to our Corps. "Damn another day in the Glorious Marine Corps, You Gotta Love it, Damn I Love this job, . . .Ah Roo Ah. Marine Corps!" These shouts, we knew motivated the recruits, and also kept them wondering what the Hell was going on with these crazy men wearing the Smokies. Admin days were designated days before our training days began. This allowed us to set the tone for the everyday living procedures for our platoons. It was basically a what to do and what not to do period of time. We would lecture procedures to the platoon. But naturally our lectures were unlike any lectures these men had ever encountered. The recruits were now on the Platoon Street with their footlockers in the proper position, Sgt Morse had arrived to assist in this introduction phase of our Admin time. While we were going over what was to be expected, the Boss would personally interview each recruit with general questions on Who, What, and Why. This allowed us to get some personal insight to each private, and would be the basis for the individual file (5x8 cards) we kept on each recruit. These cards were updated on any major infractions the recruits might have committed, as well as our general observation of their performance.

"Listen up sweeties. The Plt Cmdr will be calling out names, as a name is called you will sound off that persons name. Naturally who ever has his name called will stop what he is doing secure his gear and report to the Plt Cmdr. You will go to the duty hut and knock three times, sound off with your name which is Private what ever your last name is, requests permission to enter the duty hut. Once told to enter you will march in and center yourself not more than six inches from the desk in front of the Plt Cmdr!. Understood? "Sir Yes Sir!" "You will then sound off with Private, whatever your name is reporting as ordered Sir! Is that understood? You will be at the position of attention with your eyeballs locked straight to the front thumbs along the seams of your trousers, fingers inboard, heels together and feet at a 45-degree angle! Got that!? "Sir Yes Sir!" I now demonstrated the proper procedure for knocking on the hatch and entering the Hut. Anyone of you turds been to college? "I have Sir" "I, my ass, I told you that those holes on each side of your nose were eyes, you are a Private (E-1), the lowest rank in the Marine Corps, you are lower than whale shit!" "Sir the Private has been to college" this recruit now stated correctly. "Ok shit-for-brains, report to the Plt Cmdr, you are now our secretary, Go Asshole!"

For the next two days the recruits would be instructed on everything from how to make their racks, stow their gear, and how to properly speak or request permission to speak to a Drill Instructor. We had to cover every facet of living procedures for these men. Once a procedure was taught or a rule established, no infraction would be tolerated. They had to learn quickly and we had no time to play silly games.

Uniformity was the key to our instruction. It served to create a Team Spirit, and the Corps placed a great emphasis on teamwork. We were as a platoon or as a Corps only as strong as our weakest person. Consequently, the training at the depot was designed to test the abilities of the individual recruits, yet designed to measure those abilities as a platoon. Rewards and punishment were usually dealt on the platoon level.

Throughout this first day, all the Hats would be doing the same thing with their recruits. Morse and I conducted the various classes. The Boss could be heard correcting any mistake that the recruits may have committed when reporting to him. "What do you mean you forgot how to report, did not the Drill Instructors tell you what to do? They did? Well are you just plain fucking stupid? You're not? You just want to piss me off? Then what the fuck is the problem? You don't know!? Shit, I bet you are some kind of commie spy sent here just to fuck up my Marine Corps! Where the hell did you get all of those pimples? You are now designated as Pizza Face. Holy Shit! You gotta to have the biggest set of ears I have ever seen on one person, Dumbo Ears. You with all that shit hanging over your belt, Lard Ass." On and on these terms of endearment for various recruits would come from the Boss. He never seemed to lack any term or phrase for the recruits. "Hey Pizza face, from now on after showers you will report to the duty Drill Instructor with your wash cloth and bottle of Listerine, we are going to clear those zits off your face. If you leave here, I guarantee your face is going to be as smooth as a babies ass. I sure don't want all that zit juice squirting all over my Marine Corps Uniform. So you will wash your face with the cloth and then just like after-shave you will use the Listerine. Understood!? All of these verbal barbs were punctuated with questions of why the recruit joined the Marine Corps, his background etc. "Why did you join the Marine Corps? Son!" "Kill VC Sir!" "Oh so you think your some kind of Killer do you? Ever Kill anyone?" "No Sir." But you think you can Huh? "Sir Yes Sir!" "Well, we shall see what you are made of, now get the hell out of here!"

The interview process served to give us an idea of what we had in our platoon to work with. It helped us to get an overall impression of the type of young men we had been saddled with. Assisting us, at least initially in our selection of Squad Leaders, Platoon Guide, Secretary and probably the most important billet any recruit could be selected for that of the House Mouse. Normally, the House Mouse was selected from the smallest members of the platoon. His job was to do a general clean up of our duty hut and ensure coffee was ready. More importantly we knew that the House Mouse would become the master of gossip or as we called it scuttlebutt. Because of his unlimited access to our duty hut and gear, the mouse would be among the D.I.s when we would talk among ourselves. We knew that anything said would get back to the platoon. On many occasions we would purposely say or do things so the platoon would be aware of what was to happen or our pleasure and displeasure with their performance. This served to let the platoon iron out many of the problems before we had to get involved. We might say something like "The next time those assholes move so slow, I'm going to make them do bends and thrusts till hell freezes over!" or for motivational purposes we might tell the Boss or another Hat, "You know those scumbags seem to finally be getting their shit together." Of course the recruits did not realize we had planted these seeds purposely. After all to them we were crazy men the Marine Corps had somehow found and let loose from an insane asylum to make their lives miserable.

We had accomplished a great deal on our first full day with the herd. The Boss had interviewed each member of the Platoon, the recruits had marked all their clothing, learned how to make their racks, Marine Corps style and learned the daily routine of how to clean the area. Basically we covered the everyday chores and expectations of their daily living as a recruit on the depot. We followed four simple guidelines in our explanation of anything we wanted done. Tell them what and how to do something, demonstrate what and how to do it, then let them do it under our supervision. Most important tolerate nothing less than perfection. We did not have the luxury to coddle these people. You had to take over 80 men from different backgrounds, educational levels, volunteers and draftees. (The Marine Corps did take men from the draft pool during this timeframe), teach them everything from how to take a shower, march, speak etc., and mold them into United States Marines. This all accomplished under a very rigid timeframe. T-1 (training day -1) started in just two days. Once in the training cycle, every minute was allocated to the ultimate goal of graduating well-trained Marines.

The day had drawn to a close and I was the duty D.I., Sgt Morse would relieve me the next day. Our Squad Leaders had been selected by the boss as well as the Plt Guide and House Mouse. These billets were filled by recruits we thought had a little more smarts or maturity than the rest and were positions of responsibility within the platoon. None of the jobs were etched in stone, and we would replace these individuals if they were found lacking in any situation.

"Well Boss the herd's in the shower I ran through the how to shave drill and gave them 20 minutes to shit, shower and shave." "What kind of turds did we get this time?" He frowned and said basically the same makeup as any other platoon. The majority joined, but we do have a couple of draftees, some can actually read and write. How about that shit? Some recruiter must have really fucked up! We have our usual share of rocks, we have three with prior service 1 squid, (Navy) and two doggies (Army). I made them Squad Leaders till we see if they can handle the job. That big Mother I made the guide, so this is really no different than any other herd. Well Hernandez I'm ready to shove off, see ya about 0800 tomorrow." "Yeah Boss, have a couple for me, Semper Fi."

Twenty minutes had gone by, the recruits should now have returned from the showers and be in their Huts. "Squad Leaders!, I shouted from my seat behind our field desk, no response. "Squad Leaders Plt 3009!" I shouted again, this time my command was parroted, the recruits had not yet learned the sound of my voice.

They, in less than one week would be able to distinguish their D.I'.s voice from any other Hat on the Drill Field. We at times would attempt to stump other platoons by giving commands to them to see if they would obey, of course they had hell to pay if they listened to us. "Damn it!, I said Squad Leaders, and I better have four bodies in front of my duty hut, pretty fucking quick!" Almost immediately four voices exclaimed "Squad Leaders reporting as ordered Sir!" "You maggots! When I call for my squad leaders, I best not have to repeat myself, Understood? Get into the pits." The freshly showered squad leaders obeyed. I had them roll in and out of the sandy pit area a couple of three times. "You assholes were placed in a position of responsibility and you had better be aware of what is going on around you, do you understand? I don't care if I whisper your names, you better get your slimy asses up here. Is that Understood?" "Sir Yes Sir!" "Get up, now get out of my sight and tell the platoon to get into the classroom. They have 30 seconds. Go, Go!"

"House Mouse," I now commanded, and this time probably because they had heard the ass chewing of the squad leaders, the platoon repeated my request as they had been instructed. Very quickly a little recruit ran up and said "House Mouse reporting as ordered Sir." "OK Mouse, I want the classroom setup and this is the way it will be for me from now on. Understand? You will place three footlockers on top of each other at the entrance of the Hut. My pack of Salems placed in the left corner so I can read the name, a lighter and a cup of coffee with 99 grains of sugar placed on the upper right corner, handle facing the rear of the Hut, the cigarettes can be found in my wall locker , and you already know were the coffee is, don't you? "Sir Yes Sir." "Well than do it!" "Aye Aye Sir," the mouse said before he ran to his duties. Well at least this one turd seemed to remember what we had taught them that day. Aye Aye meant I understand the order and will comply with it.

I now entered the 1st Hut. It had been designated as the classroom earlier that day. Attention was sounded, by the recruits, they now were all standing in the classroom at the position of attention.

They had been taught when any Marine entered their quarters they had best sound off Attention. This courtesy would only be extended to Marine Officers once they entered the Marine Corps. But as with all our customs and courtesies they must first be taught and practiced in recruit training. 'Alright take your seats," Which really meant to sit down on their asses, My footlockers were in place and my Salems placed in the correct position, coffee was even where it was supposed to be. Maybe the Mouse had his shit together. I tasted the coffee and spat it out, tossing the cup across the Hut. "Mouse you piece of shit, I said 99 grains of sugar, no more and no less, this coffee has only 98 grains in it, go get me another cup and you better make damn sure its right!"

I looked at the remaining members of the platoon. "You shitheads had better understand one fucking thing Right Now. Almost good, almost clean, almost ready, is not good enough. In My Marine Corps, you either accomplish the mission or you don't. Almost is not a term we use, we do or we die trying!

We covered a lot of ground today, tomorrow is Sunday so all you fish eaters may go to church. You will be told where and when to fall out for church in the morning. If you decide to go to church understand one thing, it is your time to worship and not a time to try and screw off or catch a few extra winks of sleep. If I find out you slept in church. Then you might as well stay at church and arrange for your fucking funeral. Because your ass will be mine when you get back. One other thing, you can see our chaplain whenever you want, but don't think you can cry on the Padres' shoulder because our chaplain was a Marine Sergeant before he became a Sky Pilot. Once we have finished here, you will go back to your Huts and break out your writing materials. All of you will write home. Your mommies don't want to hear a lot of bullshit about how rough it is here. Just tell them you are alive and well, you are getting good chow and that they don't need to send any civilian shit, like cookies, candy, none of that crap. Understand? If they insist on sending you any of that shit, lets just say you won't enjoy it!

Any questions? You there! Four Eyes! what do you want?" "Sir, does the Drill Instructor think the privates will be going to Viet Nam?" "Your fucking straight you will probably be going to the Nam, you could hear a audible sucking in of 80 collective breaths, Damn it people, you should be praying to go to War. War is our business and right now business is good! As a matter of fact that will be our motivational phrase, why the hell do you think it's so important to learn everything that is being taught. This job isn't like some civilian bullshit job. When one of you screws up, somebody can get killed. We all have to work together, pull together if you want to graduate from this place. Right now I think all of you are a bunch of worthless turds, but each night we will have a classroom session, go over what you did and what you need to work on, which right at this minute is every fucking thing! Nam will come soon enough, you will have five minutes to write, than you will get ready for hygiene inspection. After that it will be time for lights out and time for you to hit the racks."

The hygiene inspection uniform is your skivvy shirt, shorts and shower shoes. You will be standing on your footlockers facing outboard, Understand? The purpose of this inspection is to see if you have any problems and will be done every night. I will walk up to you and as I pass you, you will let me know if there is any type of problem. Don't bother me with any little bullshit either, Understand?"

Once I have passed you, you will get off your footlocker, lock your lock and stand by your racks. Once I have finished with all you maggots you will hear the command prepare to mount at which point you will take your sheets and pull them back, you will than hear the command to mount, and you will get your sorry butts in the rack. I will then say one, you will pull the sheets up around your skuzzy bodies, On two you will close your eyelids, and on three you will be asleep, is that Understood?" "Sir Yes Sir!" Do It! Go, Go, Go!

Walking back to the duty hut, I saw the recruits who would be standing firewatch in front of my hatch. Like guard duty, the recruits on fire watch, were to stand a one-hour shift and walk in and out of all our platoons area. Their purpose to report any unusual activity to the

D.I. on duty. The watch rotated between all members of the platoon. "Which one of you has the 0400 to 0500 watch?" "Sir, this private has the watch." "What's your name?" "Sir Collins Sir!" "OK Collins at 0400 I want you to enter the Duty Hut, you will go to the third wall locker on the right and open it up. You will than announce the time. Do you understand? You had better not forget either. All right all of you know your time of watch and you had better know where the recruit that's suppose to relieve you sleeps. You all know that if anything takes place you will come and get me right?" "Sir, Yes Sir!" "I have no other instructions for you. So, do it!" "Aye, Aye, Sir."

Entering the duty hut, I saw three recruits down in the pushup position with Sgt. Taglieri standing over them. "Sooo . . .you turds think that classroom time is a time to just screw around, do You?" "Sir No Sir!" "Bullshit! maybe a few pushups will take some of that energy out of your skuzzy bodies, you think you're back in High School don't you?" "Sir No Sir!" "Hey, Sgt. Taglieri what do you have there?" "Oh these maggots think they can laugh and joke when they think I'm not looking." As we were speaking the other Duty D.I'.s Sgt's Perez and White walked in, since we all had a few minutes to spare before hygiene inspection, and here were three recruits in our duty hut, we all just naturally had to take turns helping Sgt. Taglieri correct his charges. "Hey Sgt. Taglieri, that big ass recruit is not staying in the pushup position." "Oh No! You want to quit on me don't you?" "Sir No Sir!" "Yes he does, look at his eyes looks like he is about to cry, poor baby wants to go home to mommy. I bet he has never been away from home. Right Shithead? We continued to help adding our own terms of endearment on each recruit. We still had to conduct hygiene inspection, so we left Sgt. Taglieri to his charges.

I entered the first hut to conduct the inspection, as instructed the group was ready and sounded attention as I entered. As I walked by each recruit I tapped him on the shoulder. And at the same time I inspected the area. "Sir no problem Sir," was parroted by each recruit as they were being tapped on the shoulder. "Sir the recruit has a problem," sounded off one recruit. "A problem what the hell is the matter with you?" "Sir the Private has a skinned knee." "OK maggot turn around and lets take a look at it. OH bullshit, my grandmother had worse scrapes than that! What are you some kind of pansy? Reach down between your legs, do you have a set of balls or What? I suppose you think you need some kind of medical attention. Since you seem to be in such pain maybe this is a medical emergency. Maybe we should call the ambulance for you! Well all right scumbag, you do seem to be in pain so I think this is an emergency, so I want you to run around the platoon area making sounds like a siren. Move it! "The private went running around the area making his siren sounds while I continued with hygiene inspection.

Completed, I finally called for Private Ambulance. That shithead was still running around sounding like an ambulance. "Well sweetie do you feel better now, I asked, "Sir Yes Sir!" Then get the fuck back to your Hut!"

"Plt 3009!" I shouted from the middle of the Plt Street. "Sir Plt 3009," "prepare to mount, Mount! One! Two! Three!" Now they had been told that on the number three they were to be asleep, so just for the hell of it I shouted "Four," no sound, Damn it, I yelled, I said Four!" Sure enough I heard from the recruits, Four Sir! "Bullshit! I told you ladies that on three you had best be asleep. If you were asleep you would not be able to hear the number Four! Get out of the racks, let's try this all over again! "It was amazing how often this ploy worked and it never ceased to amaze me.

The herd was now bedded down for the night except for the firewatches. Time for me to take it easy and get some paperwork done before I hit the rack. The boss always left a things-to-do list and we recorded the day's events for him on his little portable tape player. The duty hut would be filled with the rest of the Hats on duty. It was now our time to unwind and basically just shoot the shit about the events of the day and bullshit each other on how great our herds were doing and how bad their herds seem to be.

"Hey Hernandez you going to play firewatch tonight?" "Yeah I will probably go out about 2300. How did your turds do today?" "I don't know, I think I have a pretty good group, said Taglieri. But you know that don't mean shit at this stage of the game."

Like I said, we Hats had all different types of personalities and most of us had different jobs or Military Occupational Specialties (MOS). A Drill Instructor was what was considered to be a B billet in the Marine Corps. That is a secondary type of duty from what was your normal job assignment. Our series seemed to run the entire spectrum of different Occupational Specialties. Sgt. Taglieri our little Italian D.I., was a full fledge Grunt Infantryman all the way, Sgt. Perez was an Amtrac operator (Amphibious Vehicle Driver), Sgt. Morse was an Ammo Tech, Ssgt Navarre was an Armorer, Ssgt Yordt, was a Postal Clerk, Ssgt Bosch was another Infantryman, Ssgt Mimiaga was in Motor Transport, the Series Gunns was a wireman and the Series Officer was an Infantry Officer. I had been a grunt, but changed my duties to Administration. The different jobs didn't mean shit. Because in the Corps we have always preached that every Marine was first and foremost a basic Infantryman and the common denominator for all Marines' was Boot Camp and the D.I.'s.

For us it was not only boot camp, but also D.I. School and our loyalty to each other and the Corps. Well I finally sat down at the field desk, pulled off my Smokie and started my paperwork and in walks Ssgt Mimiaga, as always he started to bum a smoke from me. "Hey Hernandez, says Mimiaga a combination of Mexican and Yaqui Indian, how's about a smoke?" 'Damn it Mimi, don't you ever buy damn cigarettes?" "Come on Amigo, just one for the road." "Bullshit! you have not bought a pack of smokes since I have known you! Oh Right, I will give you your Cig. but you had better not keep me up all night playing fucking chess!" "Yeah, no shit" says Perez, "I need my beauty sleep!" "As fucking butt ugly as you are," says Tag, "you could sleep for the next hundred years and it wouldn't do you a bit of good!" "Fuck You Tag! Hey Hernandez what the hell were you doing with your House Mouse today? I saw the little shit with a coffee cup, he would place it on the field desk and practice snatching it up very quickly." "That's a little surprise Morse and I dreamed up for the Boss. You know how he likes his coffee and wants everything done quickly. We told the mouse if he wanted to impress the Plt Cmdr, when he asked for his usual cup of coffee that he was to snatch it up from the desk and do it faster than a greased pig. What about you Perez I saw your goats in the pits most of the day?"

We loved to get Perez going because he was so easy to get excited! "Those Mother Fuckers;" he said and then like a banty rooster he started walking up and down the Hut telling us the events that led up to him putting his recruits in the Pit. "I told that shit-for-brains Guide of mine to get the Platoon on the street and have them ready to mark their boots." Well now Perez has somewhat of an accent, so we all knew that the Guide heard the word **Butts** instead of Boots. Sure enough the platoon had fallen out on the Platoon Street in only their underwear (skivvies). Perez was now really getting into the story, yelling at the top of his lungs, "Sooo . . .I had to tell that shit-for-brains Guide, now pointing to his feet that we were to mark these boots and then to his butt not these butts!" We were all now about to die laughing as Perez continue with his "Damn straight I put their asses in the pit." Those maggots will be tighter than a frog's ass when I get done with them!"

When we were not harassing the recruits, we harassed each other and this night was typical of all our nights on duty. Sitting at the field desk, paperwork getting done, cup of coffee in hand, maybe a smoke and the constant banter and fucking with one another created a close knit group. "Well Hell," I said, "I guess I will check on the platoon and then hit the rack." "You doing the Firewatch routine?" asked Tag, "Yeah," I had gotten into the habit of pretending to be a recruit dressed as a firewatch. This trick could only be done for the first couple of nights we had the recruits. They would soon learn to recognize us no matter how dressed. The privates up to this point were still in a state of confusion and they really had no idea who the other members of their platoon were. "Remember the last herd? I had that turd that actually asked me for a light for his cigarette!" He knew full well that we didn't let any of the turds smoke unless we gave them a smoke break, and if we did they would have to smoke by the numbers. This meant that they were given a command to inhale and exhale, when this dumb shit finally realized who I was, he just fucking fainted! "Ha that was great!" I left the duty hut donning on the orange safety vest and helmet of the firewatch, and started my walk through the platoon area.

Now, the little shits were suppose to be asleep, but I knew better and the recruits thinking I was one of them would say some pretty strange things. Entering the first hut I walked around a bit, "Hey You Firewatch!" "Yeah?" "Are the D.I.s asleep yet?" "I think so!" "Man those are some crazy bastards!" "Yeah" I said, especially that Hernandez, and that Morse he really is a fruitcake" "Sure wish I could get the hell out of here I continued." "Naw those crazy bastards would probably shoot us." It was amazing the conversations I was able to hear and participate in. This little game allowed me to find out if our efforts were paying off, and had we placed the recruits in a sufficient state of shock. Had I heard this place isn't so bad or shit I thought Boot Camp was suppose to be rough, then we might have to change or tactics. It was ironic how stress or duress caused people to work and pull together. Under the conditions we had created on their first day, we knew the recruits would start pulling together in one common goal and that was to keep us, their D.I.s, from getting pissed off at them! In my opinion this stress helped weed out those recruits that would not be able to handle difficult situations. We felt it was better for them to break now then on the battlefield. Having completed my little game it was time to hit the rack and get ready for another day.

"Anything interesting happen while you were playing firewatch?" asked Sgt. Tagleri. "Same old shit, you know, most were crying about being away from home, regretting the day they were born." "Then that sounds like we had a good first day and we are doing our jobs! So what time is your firewatch holding reveille? "I told him to wake me up at 0400, I'll be ready to go by that time."

We all did things to make the privates believe we were in fact what they thought, and that was that we were out of our ever-loving minds. This thought, that maybe we were all nuts, for some reason seemed to placate the recruits and even seemed to make boot camp more tolerable. I could remember some of the antics my Drill Instructors had done, while I was in boot camp. Shit, they had no problem calling us to attention while we were climbing the ropes on the obstacle course. Naturally when you came to attention you let loose of the rope and Oh Well you just fell. I also remembered that we tried to do everything right, least we bring the anger of those unpredictable demons in Smokie the bear hats down upon us. More importantly I believe it added to the total experience of Marine Boot Camp and an overwhelming sense of accomplishment when it was finally over. Boot Camp was the common thread that wove all of us into a binding cloth, and the D.I.s guided the needle. One of the things I liked to do to help add to this idea of us being a little out of the ordinary, was to tell my firewatch how I wanted to be woken up on the first morning. I told him to enter the Duty Hut and then go to the first Wall locker on the right and open the locker's hatch. Now my own alarm clock was set thirty minutes prior to the recruit entering the duty hut. This gave me time to get up and get dressed. I then placed myself inside the wall locker Smokey and all. When the firewatch opened the hatch. I would open my eyes. And in the nicest voice I could muster, thank him for waking me up. With the added explanation that I didn't like to wrinkle my uniform. Knowing full well before the end of the day the word would be passed throughout the platoon that Sgt. Hernandez, that little crazy SOB, actually slept in a wall locker.

"Reveille, Reveille another Glorious and wonderful day to serve God, Country, and the U. S. Marine Corps!" Today was Sunday and it was really not much different than any other day on the recruit depot. Recruits were allowed to go to religious service but even these services were not spent without a D. I. One Hat in the series would march all recruits going to church and march them back. Much later in their training the recruits as part of their progression would be allowed to march themselves in squad units to church. But this would be much later, and was considered to be a privilege that had to be earned.

Sgt Morse was the duty D.I. for our platoon. By the time he arrived the recruits had already had their morning head call. Been to morning chow and were now sitting on their footlockers outside their huts, Sgt Morse would be instructing them on how to stow their gear in the footlockers, start teaching some basic drill movements left and right face, all done by the numbers. Every drill movement was broken down into parts or counts. Initially every movement was done by the numbers, we would command a count and for the count the platoon would execute that part of the movement, until they learned it sufficiently to combine the counts and execute the movements smoothly and as one person. Sgt Morse would also introduce them to their knowledge. This was a little red notebook that all recruits carried on their person. It contained a summary of just about everything they would be required to memorize in their training. When waiting to enter a class or after chow or while waiting for the rest of the platoon. the recruits were required to study this notebook constantly. "Break out your Knowledge" was a common phrase, that could be heard throughout the Depot. The idea was that as long as these young men had their nose stuck inside these notebooks it would keep them occupied and they might even learn something! Tomorrow was T-1 (Training day one) the first of 90 training days before graduation. But more importantly T-1 was also the day the recruits would be issued the one piece of equipment that was synonymous with name Marine, their rifles. Tomorrow was another day and for now Sgt Morse had the duty, so it would be my day off, Yeah day off, Bullshit! I was expected to be in anyway, but what to do with the rest of the day? Usually a day off for any hat was a day to catch up on some sleep and for us unmarried personnel another day to party hearty. My own routine was to go to my apartment and catch a few winks, get my gear ready for the next day, and then a beeline straight for the Anchor. The married personnel had their own routine, and believe me, any marriage that survived a tour on the Drill Field was, as they say, a marriage made in Heaven. You had to mentally adjust yourself to the dramatic change of being a Lion by day, giving commands, then going home and getting commands and turning into a lamb by night . . .I was truly amazed how any women could put up with the long hours we worked. Like I said the Anchor was a great place and I got there about 1900. The place was already packed, Jukebox blaring, you could find just about anything you wanted on that old box, from Country Western to Jazz and even marching songs. I found a seat at the bar and Stoney the bartender immediately put a seven seven in front of me. Not that I was a regular or anything. The area behind the bar was decorated with all types of Marine Corps memorabilia.

"Hey Tag!" I called out as I seen my buddy enter the bar, "pull it up" We sat around sipping our drinks and, as always talked about the recruits, keeping an eye open for any women that might happen to come in. "Remember that time those two shit birds came in here to try and use the damn pay phone?" "Yeah no shit!" We were recalling the time two recruits trying to go over the hill and had somehow escaped the Recruit Depot and ended up in the Anchor. They walked in baldheaded and yellow sweatshirts. You should have seen the look on their faces when they opened the door. You see many a D.I. just left work and dropped by the Anchor while still in uniform. When these turds walked in, there were more stripes at the bar then on a damn Zebra. Well of course all hell broke loose when these dips came into our bar. Imagine about 40 Drill Instructors in a bar with two recruits trying to go over the hill. It was great! The turds actually begged Stoney the bartender to call the Military Police to come get them.

We continued bullshitting until we finally surmised that nothing was going to happen in the Women department tonight. "Shit, nothing happening here tonight" Tag says. "What the hell did you expect? All the women in San Diego know you are out and on the prowl. Fucking neon sign outside says "Women beware Tag's out and about." "Kiss my Ass!" "Yeah, Semper Fi I'm outta here maybe I'll try the Marine Room," which was another bar not to far from the Anchor," maybe I will find some loose women in there. Won't do you any good, cause as butt ugly as you are you might as well just take the duty every day. You know day on stay on." "Yeah well, stay on this!" I told him, giving him the middle finger, "See Ya later," "Ooh Rah," was Tags only response. It appeared that the women of San Diego must have all decided to go to evening Mass because no luck. So I just went back to my place and hit the rack.

According to the training schedule, rifle issue was at 0900, so I went straight to the Armory. The platoon was standing at attention, their noses buried in their knowledge. The boss had the squad leaders down in the pushup position, Shit! the squad leaders had already pissed off the boss, not a good sign. "Hey boss what's up I asked?" "These maggots don't want to keep their jobs very long. I came in early and my old grandmother moves faster than these maggots. On your feet ladies!" shouted the boss to the squad leaders, "rejoin your squads. Move!" "Listen up" shouted Sgt. Morse, "we will now be issued our weapons by squad. Once you receive your weapon you will sound off your name and rifle number to Sgt. Hernandez, your rifle number is located on the rear of your weapon." Sgt Morse now showed the entire platoon the location of this number. "This number will be memorized and you had better know this number when asked." We continued with the issue of weapons, naturally many a recruit screwed up the procedure of sounding their name and weapon number. "What the fuck is a matter with you Dumbo Ears? You are just one plain fuck up, aren't you?" "Sir No Sir!" "Bullshit in just two days you have screwed up just about everything you have tried. I'm keeping an eye on you, I strongly suggest you get your shit together and you had better do it very quickly!" The entire platoon had now been issued the rifles, "OK sweeties, says the boss, you will always refer to your M-14 as a rifle or weapon never ever a gun. Your gun is between your legs, your weapon is what you now have and it has one purpose in life and that is for killing, your gun is for fun, is that Understood? If you turds make it to the rifle range you will be instructed on its deadly use. That is still along way off, first we must become familiar with the weapon, not only its nomenclature and characteristics, but also in the manual of arms and that ladies is done on the parade deck."

The parade deck, field or grinder made up a great deal of our training time and drill unlike many of the other classes the recruits would receive, e.g. first aid, history, close combat etc, was the sole responsibility of the D.I.s. We took a great deal of pride in our ability to teach drill movements, and the many hours spent on the grinder allowed us to observe each and every recruit. "You people listen up, the purpose of drill is to move units from one location to another in an orderly fashion. It also is the basis from which you can be deployed into different combat formations. That's what the manual says, Now get this through your heads, drill allows all of you to move like one person, teamwork is the key, each movement will be explained demonstrated and divided into its basic components. It will be practiced over and over, until it is done perfectly and in unison. Now I want you to look around Do it! See those other platoons? They are preparing for their final drill competition. That means they will be graduating pretty soon. Maybe, just fucking Maybe, you maggots will be able to march like them. Bullshit, you will be better than they are, you will be a green machine, a fucking precision instrument, moving like one person! Do You Understand? Grinder time or drill periods was one period where all three of us were always present. We watched every move and no infraction went unnoticed or uncorrected.

The Boss's speech had really motivated the privates, but they would soon realize that time spent on the grinder added up to very hard work, and that we would watch them like hawks. Soon they were practicing each movement over and over again, and we were correcting any minor flaws in the execution of the drill movements. "Jesus can't you people get your shit together, this is your left and this is your right, I told you 40 inches back to chest, No! No! do it again girls, and if you can't get it right maybe a little pit time will help you learn!" The barrage of verbal correction was unending and we knew that our time was limited. In my opinion training the recruits was no different than training a boxer for a championship bout, first he had to be broken down, then built back up, both physically and mentally. The trainers had to bring him to that razor's edge of preparedness, and the Corps did the same thing with its recruits. Our training syllabus was designed to prepare the recruits for the three major milestones of boot camp. The first would be their initial drill competition, personnel inspection, then the rifle range and final events, and then graduation. At this stage of the game the recruits resembled a bunch of hodge podge sad sacks, or as we liked to say "Bags of shit with bodies in them." Their covers were not fitted properly, belts too long, just a bunch of wrinkles, they in no way looked like a spit and polished Marine. But they would, they certainly would! It was truly amazing to watch the transformation process of these young men. That hodge podge sack-of-shit look would disappear more and more as each day went by. We of course, helped this process, instructing them in the proper way to wear their uniforms from cover to boots, even the right way to lace their shoes, left over the right. Each item of the uniform or piece of equipment not only had its own place but also had its own ritual. Naturally the more items they had been instructed on, the more items we had to correct. As always, the corrections were constant and plentiful. "Hey you numb nuts! Some body sit on you head? block that cover, No, No, I told you maggots the only time you wear your covers was outside, what the fuck you shine those boots with a Hershey Bar?" One of the major infractions on the uniform items were what we called Irish pennants. Any piece of thread hanging no matter how small from the uniform, "You worthless piece of shit, that can't possibly be a Irish pennant I see, Get down in the push up position," "How Many Sir?" "How Many!, Well smart ass you do pushups' until my arms hurt! Understand?"

As the training progressed, the days seemed to all run together, each day governed by the training schedule. Before we realized it about six weeks had already gone by and it was time to prepare the platoons for their first formal inspection and their initial drill competition. We had almost reached the half way point in our the training syllabus. This particular group had fared fairly well. We had only dropped or lost five of the original members of the platoon. Two were dropped because of injuries received on the obstacle course, they would be recycled into other platoons who were at the same training day the recruits had been prior to their being injured. The other three recruits had been sent to our motivation platoon.

Motivation was a separate training section on the Depot. This was where we sent those privates that needed that little extra push to help them change their overall attitude. The Moto platoon could be seen periodically throughout the Depot, they were easily recognized because of the helmets they wore, rather than the standard cover of the other recruits, they also carried 10 pound sledgehammers, rather than the rifles the recruits carried. Their daily training consisted of mainly physical training, running, obstacle course, drill and as we liked to say making little rocks out of big ones, e. g. the sledge hammers. All of their training was conducted under D.I.s assigned to the Motivation Section. Just the threat of sending a recruit to the motivation section, usually served to take care of any attitude problem the recruit might have! Normally motivation was the last resort the Marine Corps would take to keep a recruit in the Corps. Some individuals just could not adjust to the radical change from civilian life to life on the depot and subsequently in the Marine Corps. Those that Moto could not help would be discharged from the Corps as undesirable for Military Service. A classification that would follow them for the rest of their lives. We just called them "Shit Birds that were to gutless too defend their own country and left it at that!

We were now at that stage of training where the recruits had mastered the everyday living procedures on the recruit depot. Giving us the time to concentrate on refining the instruction they had already received. Don't doubt for one minute that anything less than perfection was tolerated. The recruits knew damn well that we would put them in the pits in a heartbeat if they screwed up. They had received instruction in First Aid, History, Bayonet Training. They had run the obstacle course and had mastered the assembly and disassembly of their weapons, most of the drill movements had been taught and they even looked half ass decent. They had the daily routine of living and cleaning up down pat. Virtually when to sleep, eat, shower and yes even when to take a shit. Now that they were almost at the half way point of training, the recruits now had to prove they had mastered the training they had received to date. In the Corps this meant only one thing and that was examination and inspection.

The upcoming days would become almost as hectic to the recruits and us as the first few days of boot camp. We had to prepare them for their first series of tests, their first inspection and of course initial drill competition. This would close phase I of our training syllabus. Yeah, life was good and besides this was not anything we had not done before.

"House Mouse!" I called and the platoon responded by instantly repeating my call, almost as quickly I heard the three distinct knocks at my hatch with "House Mouse reporting as ordered Sir!" House Mouse you little turd, why is my shit can (trash), still full of trash, drop down and give me 50!" "Sir Aye Aye Sir!" I sat back in my chair, coffee in hand while the mouse counted his 50 push-ups. This was the start of the phase of training that I most enjoyed! "Sir fifty Sir, and one for the Corps Sir" "Get the hell out of my sight you little turd, and make sure my shit can is never full again Understand? Move it!" The Mouse just like the rest of the platoon was finally at that stage where he understood what had to be done and how to do it. But for now the recruits were in the sack and I had a hot cup of coffee in one had and a cig in the other and could sit back and relax while the other Hats filed into the Duty Hut.

Each platoon was given to different mistakes and we had different methods of correcting the privates. Each evening gave us the opportunity to talk about our herds, evaluate what they had done or failed to do, you know just sit around and bullshit with the other hats. Our idea of winding down after a day with the recruits was to harass each other and talk about some of the silly stunts our privates had pulled. "Hey Hernandez, your platoon sure looked ragged today!" "Bullshit!" I said to Tag, "compared to that mob of yours, mine could be the Marine Corps Drill Team." "Both of you are full of shit," chimed in Perez "my platoons tighter than a frogs ass and when it comes time for drill comp they are going to leave the rest of the series eating dust." "Fuck You Perez!" we both said together. "We've seen your mob march, looks like the fucking Salvation Army Band." "Kiss My Ass!" "Hey did your boss tell you what Morse did to the new Series Officer? He actually chased his ass right out of the D.I.s Head!" "Naw!" "Yeah he did". Seems like Morse went to the head to take a crap. And didn't know that we were going to get a new Series Officer. Anyway Morse goes into the Head and here is the lieutenant, he only had a towel wrapped around him. Well he is really young looking, so Morse thinks its somebody's recruit sneaking into the D.I's Head. So Morse screams at the LT. "What the hell do you think your doing in the D.I.s Head, you maggot, you have two fucking seconds to get out of this Head and out of my sight!" Well the LT doesn't even bat any eye, He just says Aye Aye Sir, and gets the hell out of the head. "You're bullshitting us." "No Way, not ten minutes later the series GySgt takes Morse to the Company Office to meet the New L.T., Morse walks in and almost fucking chokes when he sees the L.T., and realizes this was the person he had just thrown out of the Head. The L.T. just stands up and shakes his hand and says nice to meet you Sergeant. How about that shit! I think this Officer is going to be a good one. I mean he could have fucking let Morse have it and give him a good ass chewing, but he was a good Joe about it. Looks like the type to sit back and think things out before jumping to any conclusions. Names LT. Kennedy, we are all suppose to meet him tomorrow morning and the Series Gunny says not to pull any cheap shit or he will have our balls."

"Hey Hernandez! what the hell happened to your squad leaders this morning, they were outside the Head and they all looked like they were about to puke?" Laughing I told them about my secret in teaching the recruits to clean the heads. I had taken all of my squad leaders into the head and told them that it had best be clean enough to eat from. I then showed them what I wanted and then put them in charge of making sure that the cleanup detail did it right. Well after they thought the head had been cleaned to their and my satisfaction, I had sneaked back into the head and put some peanut butter under one of the commode seats. "Well squad leaders is the head ready for inspection?" I asked? "Sir Yes Sir!" "And it has been cleaned to the standards I set earlier?" "Sir Yes Sir!" "Well let's just go see." I started the inspection and then went to the shitter I had put the peanut butter on. "What the hell is this?" I screamed. "You maggots told me the head was clean! Did I not tell you this had better be cleaner than your Mommys kitchen, clean enough to eat from, Right! Well I don't believe it, Open your Mouths! I took the peanut butter and put some in each of their mouths, their eyes got bigger than a stomped on bullfrog, they turned green around the gills, and acted like they wanted to puke. I walked out and said "from now on this head had better be fucking spotless." It works every time and that's why when we have a Head Inspection, we always pass with flying colors. I wasn't going to tell you my secret but your platoons need all the help they can get!"

"Talk about puking, remember that last platoon. we were on the PT field (Physical Training) and were just about done with our first 3 mile run, Tag was running drag, picking up the stragglers and this one goat just kept dropping out, Tag says "What's a matter with you sweetie, you had best keep up." "Sir the private thinks he is going to puke!" "Puke? You had best not dirty my Marine

Corps ground with any of your puke!" "Well this private starts to vomit, Tag yells at him again, I fucking told you, that you best not puke on my PT field!" So this turd starts to upchuck his breakfast, but following directions he opens his skivvy shirt and pukes inside. Well not one drop touched the ground. Tag did not miss a beat, Oh so you think you are some kind of genius, well you still wasted good chow! so right then and there Tag makes this private drop into the sandy area and roll around, you could hear the squashing sound of that vomit and grit as he rolls around in the sand. He only rolled around for a couple of minutes and then Tag says Get up you shit-for-brains! Well you know that turd gets up and catches the platoon and finished the run with no problem. How about that?"

"These turds can always come up with some weird shit! I don't know where they come from but everytime I have to take a herd for their first shower they have to be taught the proper shower procedure. You Know! Wash your face then your ass, some of these shitheads still insist on doing it ass backwards. I caught my dips talking the other day in the showers, they thought I had gone to the duty hut, well even after all this time, they were carrying on like they were at some silly girls school, I made them get asshole to bellybutton. So you want to act like little kids as soon as my back is turned, Is that Right? All right then grab a hold of each other and like the little girls you were acting like, we will play follow the leader. So I just made them walk around the shower area, with only the cold water on, well eighty recruits does not give much room to maneuver and we played this silly game for about ten minutes and you could see they did not like this shit at all. Bet they never screw off again when my back is turned."

"Well at least we're almost at the halfway point with this herd, I can't believe how quick the time seems to have gone by." "In just another week we will be going to the Range and I hear when we get back the Brass will have us in the new Barracks. I think I'm going to miss the old Quonset Huts, You know they put an area as the duty hut in each squad bay of the barracks so we can always be with the turds." "They probably got smart and heard about our

Bullshit sessions and decided to put a squelch on all the lies you assholes tell!" "One things for sure the next few days will keep us hopping, you know getting ready for all the initial testing." "Yeah, day on stay on will be the order of the day." "This really puts a dent in my love life." "Shit, the only love life you have is that right hand of yours, even named it five finger Mary!" "Kiss My Ass! Let me tell you something there are a lot of broken hearts in San Diego, every time I have the duty." "Yeah Sure! Semper Fi." "Its time to hit the rack," says Tag," and dream about all of those sweet things that are safe for one more night since I have to be here with the rest of you JarHeads." Of course his comment just brought a chorus of Fuck You's and a mass of boots flying throughout the Duty Hut.

"Sir the time on Deck is 0400, Aye Aye Sir," as with every morning till the recruits graduated the D.I.'s alarm clock was the duty firewatch announcing our wake up call. We normally awoke at least an hour before reveille allowing us time to shower, shave and get in uniform before the recruits woke up, at 0500. At exactly 0500 every morning the sounds of reveille could be heard throughout the Depot, a chorus of trumpets would sound over the loud speaker announcing to the world that another day had begun. Unlike the first week I did not have to physically go from one Hut to the other, waking up my charges. The recruits now knew the routine and I merely had to stand outside my duty hut and command "Lights on hatches open!" followed by eighty screaming voices echoing my command. They had even progressed to the point of being allowed to make head calls on their own during the evening. They knew that from the time they woke up they had exactly 10 minutes to make a head call, have their racks made, dressed and prepared to be in platoon formation on our command. This routine had not come easy, but the constant prodding , yelling and more than one pit call certainly had a way of stimulating even the slowest private. As I said, the pit was nothing more than a sandy area outside the Huts and a pit call was usually 10 to 15 minute of nothing but continuous exercises in this area, of course we were creative and might have the recruits make it Rain! We had the recruits roll in and out of the Sand, Dive into it, and then, lying face up, have the platoon throw sand up in the air or as we called it make it Rain! In most cases this made the area look as if a small sandstorm had somehow entered the Depot. We were only as good or as fast as the weakest or slowest recruit, and the platoon soon learned that if one recruit was late the entire platoon would suffer. This caused the faster ones to help the slower ones, we stressed teamwork over and over. A Marine is never alone as long as there is another Marine to help out. A Marine is never left behind, A Marine does not fuck over another Marine, and a Marine takes responsibility for his actions.

"Hey Boss! platoon's about ready, and acting like a bunch of broads going on their first date." The day for our initial drill competition and personnel inspection had finally arrived. This was the way it was with every platoon and I guess you could not blame the turds one bit for their excitement. Up to this point they platoon had looked like a shit sandwich. Our term for someone in uniform who basically looked like shit. You know, wrinkled uniform, not fitting properly. So for the last few days we had been preparing them for the Inspection and we had spent as much time as possible getting their uniforms ready. The only uniform they had to date was that of the utility uniform and we had taken their best set to the laundry for pressing and starching. We had shown them how to properly starch and block their covers, a method of taking liquid starch and actually painting it on the cover then with an array of clothes pins block each crease so that it was nice and square, with irons we brought from home we had ironed the covers. Their Web belts had been cleaned and washed in the showers during the recruits shower time and scrubbed for the last two weeks with soap and toothpaste, making them their whitest, clothing was remarked and their boots had been spit shined. All these little tidbits taught by the D.I.'s. The regulations said boots need only be buffed to a high shine. But no Marine worth his salt would just buff anything if the damn thing could be spit shined than it damn sure was spit shined. And that shine had best be good enough to tell what color skivvies some gal might be wearing if she happen to stand over them. Or more precisely, like a diamond in a goat's ass.

They were on edge, this would be the first time the recruits would be inspected by anyone other than their own D.I.'s. We tried hard to instill the importance of inspections into the privates by all the fuss and extra attention we placed on the proper fit of their uniforms and what to do during the inspection.

The inspection would be done by the Company Commander, Series Officer and our Series Gunnery Sergeant, followed by an even more detailed inspection by the Platoon Commanders of the Series. Not only would the recruits' uniforms be inspected but their knowledge would also be tested. Questions could range from First Aid to Military History, and they would be critiqued on their ability to execute the Manual of Inspection Arms with their weapons. The weapons had best be cleaned and ready to go. We had made the recruits practice Inspection Arms during hygiene inspection, taking advantage of any useable time. As we passed each recruit during hygiene inspection, he would execute inspection arms and would be tested on his knowledge.

We followed the old adage that practice makes perfect. We wanted the recruits to make a good showing in front of our Company Commander, but yet not too good at this stage of our training. We did not want the privates to think that they had nothing more to worry about. We also knew that regardless of how well the recruits performed in front of the Company Commander and Series Officer, that the Platoon Commanders would basically tear them new Assholes. No complacency would be allowed to overcome the recruits.

"Platoon 3009 on the road!" "Sir Plt 3009 on the road Aye Aye Sir," within a matter of seconds the platoon was on the road and in formation ready to go. It was my turn to take the platoon out for their initial drill competition. Not only would the recruits be graded on their performance. But I also would be graded on my conduct of the drill movements that the platoon would be asked to perform. These movements could be any drill movement the recruits were expected to know at this stage of their training. The drill competition took place on the parade deck.

"OK sweeties today is our drill competition so let's do it. Forward March! All the way to the grinder I would be trying to motivate the platoon to their best performance. "You know what's expected of you, you are not those non marching pukes, you where just a few weeks ago, you look like a machine, A Green Machine, A well oiled green machine all parts working together, Understand!" "Sir Yes Sir!" "A fucking green machine, flawless in its performance, we will be number one platoon, Women will see you and scream, kids will love you, old ladies will love you. The whole damn Recruit Depot will stand back in awe and say that Plt 3009 should be on the fucking Marine Corps Silent Drill Team, is that Understood? I can't hear you! "Sir Yes Sir!"

They were now motivated and ready to perform, yet nothing I could say would get them going as the ritual they were about to be allowed to perform. "Platoon Halt! Ok sweeties reach in you pockets and break out your blousing bands, you will now blouse your trousers, bloused between the 3rd and 4th eyelets of your boots, I will show you the proper way, Pizza Face you will be my dummy." Once instructed in the proper way to blouse their boots the platoon executed the ritual. You see the blousing of trousers is almost like a passage into manhood for the recruits. To date they were not allowed to blouse their trousers, which is nothing more than giving the appearance of trousers tucked into your boots, but you must understand the only people that had their trousers bloused were Marines, and those recruits that had completed their initial drill competition. If your trousers were not bloused then you were announcing to the rest of the world that you were a new guy, therefore a non-marching piece of shit! So now the platoon was really motivated. "Fall In!" We went through all the movements and allowed time for the evaluators to do their thing. I told the Platoon that they had done well. when it was all done but not to think for one minute that it was over. We still had the personnel inspection to go through. "OK ladies you will not be asked any questions you have not had the opportunity to receive instruction on. So I don't want to hear any" the Private does not know."

Because that is just plain bullshit. If you don't know its because your just plain fucking ignorant, so your answer had best be "The private has been instructed but fails to remember," then we will deal with your lack of memory later, Understood! We will find out the results of the drill competition later, right now you had better concentrate on the inspection, like I said you did all right, I have seen better and I have seen worse." We marched back to the company area and could see the entourage of Inspectors waiting for us.

"Sir the Platoon is prepared for Inspection," I informed the company Commander" "Accompany me in the inspection, Sergeant" he replied. The Captain (0-3), went down the line of recruits and stopped in front of each recruit in the rank he had chosen to inspect. As the inspector stopped in front of the recruit he executed Inspection Arms, and answered the questions asked of him. The Series Officer and Series Gunnery Sergeant also assisted the Company Commander in the inspection. This allowed all of them to evaluate not only the recruit's performance but also how well we had done our jobs. The recruits held the members of the Inspection Team in awe, up to now they had seen but rarely had spoken to any member of the inspection team. This was as it should be, because even if all members of the team were in the recruit's chain of command, the first person in their chain was their D.I. This was a lesson that would also follow them into the regular Marine Corps; follow the chain of command. We were not members of some civilian organization that needed to run to the boss for every little problem. The rank structure in the Marine corps was there for a purpose and that was to establish overtly that person who was an immediate supervisor. We knew that rank should be earned and in most cases those who carried the title also carried all the leadership skills to support the rank.

The Platoon Commanders had been standing by while the Company Commander and his staff conducted the inspection. They also had been making mental notes as to which recruits had screwed up in front of the Company Commanders. The inspection party left and the recruits seemed to breathe a sigh of relief, but this would be short-lived. The Company Commanders Inspection was really just a walk through, now came the detailed inspection by the Platoon Commanders.

"Oh NO NO I can't believe you told the Company Commander that you did not know your 5th general order. And look at this rifle, the fucking thing is filled with dirt and shit!" screamed Navarre, he reaches and turns the recruit's cover backwards, all the Plt Commanders were now reading the privates the riot act. The verbal jibes might be different but all had the same gist behind them. The recruit had screwed up and embarrassed themselves, their platoon, their D.I.s, and the entire Marine Corps. They had let us down, more importantly their platoon had been let down. The verbal insults were something to listen too, "Your parents did not have any children that lived! You are a fucking commie spy sent here to screw up my Marine Corps, A fucking rock has more brains then you do, You don't have enough sense to wipe your own ass, I think you are the most worthless turd I have ever seen!" All these terms of endearment just kept going on and on, the rest of the Hats and myself enjoyed watching the bosses do their thing and had to fight to keep from laughing. Naturally, most of the recruits that had screwed up were sent to the pit to contemplate the error of their ways, while doing bends and thrusts or pushups forever, or so they were told. Those that remained in the ranks looked like a tornado had gone through the Platoon. Some had their covers turned round backwards and pulled down completely covering their ears, others had their web belts wrapped around their necks like scarves, others had parts of rifles sticking out from their trousers, shirts, even the operating rod springs dangling from ears like so many ear rings. Those whose weapons had not be cleaned properly resembled Indians with War Paint, the carbon built up in the weapons formed a grit that now had been wiped on the recruits faces. Those recruits who had responded in a baby-type voice, had their trousers down around their ankles and were sucking their thumbs, reciting 'Mommy Mommy' I will soon be home'.

The detailed inspection by the Plt Cmdrs finally came to an end and we started herding the recruits back into formation with our own terms of endearment and none too soon because all of a sudden Ssgt Mimiaga sounds off with "Series Attention!" Naturally we all popped to attention. Our Battalion Commander had come to the area, A Lt Colonel (0-5), of Marines accompanied by the Battalion Sgt Major. Sergeant Major and Master Gunnery Sergeant (E-9). Is the highest enlisted rank that can be achieved. "Good Morning Sir," Sgt Tagleri, and myself said in unison while executing our salute to the LtCol. We of course added a greeting to the SgtMaj. "Looks like you just finished your initial inspection and drill?" "Yes Sir we parroted, but we were on pins and needles because the SgtMaj was approaching a large trash can very near the platoons in formation.

"Now this trash can contained one sorry ass recruit. During the Company Commanders portion of the inspection. He had asked one of the privates to tell him what time 1 PM was in military time. This shithead without batting an eye told him he still did not know how to tell military time, of course the correct answer was 1300. Well, with this answer the Boss just naturally zeroed in on this turd, and just like a rocket when the Company Commander left, the Boss was on this turd like stink on shit. In a very soft tone he told this recruit, "time and time again we have tried to teach you how to tell military time, but you just don't seem to give a shit. Right!" "Sir No Sir!" "The private just can't keep those numbers in the privates head." "Bullshit! Secretary!" the boss had screamed, "take a piece of paper and starting with 2400 I want you to write the corresponding civilian time, Understand!" Now you, You maggot I think we should just shit can you!" "That's just what the fuck I'm going to do, Get in that shit can! now, shit-for-brains, every time I hit the can you will pop up like the fucking clown that you are and announce the time, first in civilian time then in military time Understand!"

The recruit got in the can put the lid over the top and naturally we all took turns banging the can watching this turd go up and down like a jack in the box. "The SgtMaj was fast approaching this trash can." "SgtMaj!" spoke the Battalion Commander, are you ready to shove off? At the sound of the Battalion commanders voice the SgtMaj spun around and bigger than shit accidentally hit the trash can, and bigger than life up pops this recruit. "Sir the time on deck is 1PM or 1300 and then goes back into the can. The LtCol looks at the SgtMaj and says "What the heck was that?" The SgtMaj had been around awhile and had been a hat so he knew the drill, but this method of instruction was not exactly in the standard operating procedures for recruit training and we all knew we were screwed. "Sooo," says the LtCol, "I wonder how that private got into the trash can, bet none of you Drill Instructors know and if I asked the recruit I bet he would say he somehow fell in and just had the urge to recite military time. SgtMaj, you know it never ceases to amaze me how so many recruits get themselves in such weird situations." "Beats me too Sir," says the SgtMaj with a gleam in his eye. "I'm very sure that he will be out of there very soon, let's go get some chow SgtMaj. Gentleman have a good day." "Aye Aye Sir" we replied as we executed our salutes. The Old Man then started to walk away, but turns around and gives the shit can a good kick. Just like before the private pops up and announces the time on deck, the Battalion Commander just walks away shaking his head.

"Get the hell out of that can and get in platoon formation!" yells Ssgt Navarre, "Hurry up you worthless turd!" I Screamed, with Sgt Morse also threatening to put him back in the can for the rest of his life if he did not move any quicker. We all knew that the Old Man had given us a break, no harm had been done to the recruit, but sometimes a person can't see the forest through the trees and he could have made a big deal out of this incident.

The Old Man was fair, but was also very hard on any Hat that abused his fairness or took advantage of the awesome power we had over our recruits. Today's actions by the Battalion Commander just served to increase our loyalty and respect for him. This was a very shrewd move on his part, he had played us like we in turn played our House Mouse. He knew that the word would be spread among his Drill Instructors about what he had done. The Anchor would be full of talk about how he was not out to get us and understood the job of the D.I.s. The SgtMaj would ensure that we did not mistake his actions for any type of leniency, but for what they were, that of a good Officer understanding his men and their mission.

The Marine Corps took great pains to ensure that only qualified individuals became D.I.'s. However even with the screening process, some Marines became Hats, who had no reason to be in this job. Not only could they not handle the job, more importantly they could not handle the power. A Marine Drill Instructor has an unbelievable amount of power over his recruits. He possesses a control that even increases as the training cycle progresses. Truly, you are a God in your control, over these young men.

Not all the methods of training or disciplining the recruits were sanctioned by the Marine Corps and its regulations, consequently there were many do's and don'ts of what could be done to discipline a recruit. The acceptable method of disciplining a private was normally in the form of physical exercise. This too regulated by Marine Corps regulations. As to the number and type of exercises a recruit could perform at any one time. Mostly the numbers were ignored. Besides, it did not have the same effect to tell a recruit "OK maggot you will do 50 pushups and 20 bends and thrusts" It seemed to be much more effective to say "OK maggot you will do pushups till my arms get tired or bends and thrusts till hell freezes over."

Like I said, a Drill Instructor had a power that is difficult to imagine and because of that power a Hat could do just about what he wanted and in most cases their was slim chance of discovery by the Marines higher up the chain of command. Consequently, we had to police ourselves. There were forms of discipline or the abuse of power that we would not tolerate from any Hat. When discipline was given it was administered much like a Parent administers punishment to their children that may have displayed conduct that was not acceptable, and just like some parents who carried their authority too far, we had some Hats that did the same. Creating mental stress by our yelling and verbal insults were considered to be part of the job. However, physical abuse to the point of hurting a private was not tolerated and was reported up the chain of command. Incidents of extreme harm to a recruit were the exception rather than the rule. When discovered, a Hat could face dire consequences to his military career. The Marine Corps was not immune to outside criticism, and it seemed that any incident of abuse caused the Corps to come into the limelight and its training methods evaluated by the public. The Marine Corps never back pedaled from owning up to its responsibility and always seemed to answer all questions regarding its methods honestly and as quickly as possible.

If a Hat a screwed up then we said so and took corrective measures on the individual or individuals concerned. One old SgtMaj had given me some very good advice prior to my becoming a D. I . . ."If you must discipline a recruit, never ever do it while angry, with the power that you have this emotion of anger, unchecked, can very easily get out of control and cause you do something you will regret". You must become the best actor possible, and check all your emotions from humor to pity and if possible think all things out".

Not condoned by Headquarters Marine Corps but acceptable to us was the choke. A quick grasp with your hand to the recruit's neck and a quick squeeze worked wonders for immediate corrective action. This was done without malice and was not intended to make the recruits pass out or hurt him, just a quick squeeze and in our opinion done much like a parent spanking a child. As cruel as it may appear to outsiders, the choke actually became to many recruits a merit badge. We did not hesitate to administer a choke or two and the phrase of "Come closer you piece of shit so I won't have to reach so far to choke you" was quite common in the Duty Hut.

Once again in the Duty Hut, I yelled out for the House Mouse, almost immediately there was a pounding on my hatch " Sir, House Mouse reporting as ordered Sir." "Mouse get the classroom ready, tell the guide I want every swinging dick in the classroom in five minutes.

"Aye Aye Sir." I don't fucking believe it! Tag growled as he walked into the Duty Hut, that bunch of turds of yours took first in the Drill Comp. "Bullshit! I told you my herd would take first, Morse and the Boss are already at the Anchor, collecting on their bets." "Yeah! We will see how your platoon does at the Range. No way will your goats beat mine, I have nothing but John Waynes in my platoon, as a matter of fact I think you owe me a couple of cold ones from the last herd we had." "My ass! I already paid up, but you were so shitfaced and in love with that ugly broad on the barstool, you don't remember. Well as much as I would like to stay here and shoot the shit I have work to get done. The bus for the range leaves at 0700, and Boss says he wants all of our shit packed and ready to go. Did you hear about that Asshole over in first battalion, stupid son of a bitch got court martialed, he told his turds that they had to pay to get on the bus taking them to the range. Charged each one of his turds two bucks, somehow the other Hats in his series found out about it and turned his sorry ass in! He was busted from Sergeant to Private and got kicked out of the Corps with a Dishonorable Discharge." "Ah Ohh Rah", Tag Said, "worthless turds like that give us and the Corps a bad reputation. Every time some shithead like that screws up, Headquarters takes notice, it won't be long till they put an Officer with every platoon and maybe even brief the privates on the do's and don'ts of what a Hat can do!" "Yeah maybe even one day we won't even be able to yell or use foul language, because it might hurt the little sweeties ears! Look what happen last month the privates can't even say "Kill" on the bayonet course, still hard for me to believe."

"You two are talking out your asses!" Perez had come in and overheard our conversation," No way that will ever happen! Well we, of course just gave him the universal sign of endearment, the middle finger!

"Platoon Attention!" was called out as I entered the classroom, the Mouse had learned his job quite well, my 3 footlockers were stacked, pack of Salems were where they were supposed to be, and as I tasted the coffee, I told the Mouse it was acceptable to my sensitive palate. "At Ease! Be Seated! I don't know how the hell your worthless turds did it, but you took the Drill Comp and the Series Officer said he was pleased with the inspection, which by Marine Corps standards means you passed by no more that a cunt's hair." The recruits now let out a series of 'Ah Roo Ah's,' "Maybe, just Maybe, you maggots might make it out of here, but today was just a milestone in your training. We leave for the range in the morning at Camp Pendleton, Secretary, we will need a whole shitpot full of Platoon rosters, "Sir, Yes Sir!" "Guide, you had best be on your toes because we won't have time to screw around in the morning. As for the rest of you maggots don't think that you have it made in the shade, because now we are really going to start to train. Understand?!"

PHASE II
THE RANGE

Reveille had now come and gone and I knew what the recruits were feeling. We had loaded up in the big green Marine Corps buses right after morning chow, and now we were traveling down the interstate towards Camp Pendleton. Our trip was only about 25 miles, but this was the first time the recruits had been outside the confines of the Recruit Depot since joining the Corps. I had instructed them to sit at the position of attention and not eyeball the area, but you could not help but notice the city of San Diego and the houses on the surrounding hillsides or the other vehicles traveling on the interstate. All of this was part of a civilian world that they were no longer part of.

I remember how I had felt on the same trip only a few years earlier, wondering what the hell I had done. I could see all that I had been a part of and the memories of my life before Boot Camp had come flooding back. I was sure that the same type of memories was now coming back to my recruits. Traveling in a green bus with the only person already a Marine in the bus other than the driver happen to be a crazy person (my D.I.). I smiled because now I was that crazy man!

It was not unusual as we motor convoyed to Camp Pendleton to have a civilian vehicle pull along side our bus and start honking its horn. It could be a bunch of long hair's waving the peace sign and yelling vulgarities or former Marines giving us the thumbs up. This was still the era of the Hippie movement and Anti-War demonstrations. It always angered me that these assholes would yell and do such stupid things. Many of the young men in the bus might not survive the war and here these Assholes were mocking them.

We viewed these pukes as nothing but a bunch of Draft Dodgers with no balls to serve their country. I sometimes wanted to tell the bus driver to pull over, and show these long-haired pukes what a platoon of well trained recruits could do to them and their peace signs. But our orders were very clear, let them exercise their constitutional rights and just ignore them and make sure our recruits did the same. Ironically many of these young men not more than eight weeks earlier came from the same group of people who now seemed to mock them. I could hear the whispered words of "I would like to butt-stroke that asshole, no balls to defend their own country, long haired hippie pukes!" "Knock it off," I yelled, "those cocksuckers have no sense of discipline, loyalty, honor or pride. They have a right to their own opinions and that's what we do for a living sweeties, defend our rights not just for us, but for everyone. It's hard when you see these assholes. But that's just the way it is, besides they have no fucking idea what we are all about and they never will, you are special breed of cat in the eyes of the world, and we don't need them any fucking way, Right Sweeties!" "Ah Roo Ah!" was the deafening response.

"OK, sweeties off the bus, Guide!" "Sir Guide reporting as ordered Sir!" "I want the platoon formed by our Seabags," "Aye Aye Sir!" "OK you turds look around you, you are now on Marine Corps Base Camp Pendleton California, specifically Edson Range. Named after Col Edson of the Edson Raiders form World War II, you remember your history Right?" "Sir, Yes Sir!" "Everything you see is Marine Corps Property over 25 thousand acres, here is where you will learn your marksmanship training and, as a result, become the most feared military machine in the entire world. Nothing, I mean nothing can overcome a Marine and his rifle. Understood! You will qualify with your weapon and I mean you had best qualify, but first you shitheads are getting the opportunity to skate for a week. We have been assigned Mess and Maintenance with half the platoon working in the Mess Hall the other on Maintenance duty, which is really the Marine Corps way of saying cutting the grass, repairing targets and all around clean up. The Plt Commander and Drill Instructor Sgt Morse will be here in 60 minutes and I want everything ready to go by the time they arrive. When I give you the word you will get your gear, House Mouse you are responsible for setting up the duty hut, OK that's our squad bay, Now do it!"

This would now be our home for the next three weeks. The recruits would now be housed in barracks rather than the Quonset huts they had been in on the Recruit Depot. A barracks is nothing more than a large building with a big open area that could accommodate over 100 recruits in one common living area, our platoon was now under one roof, showers and head facilities in the same area. This was like moving from a tent to the Hilton Inn. But the recruits enthusiasm would be short-lived because the duty hut, our office, was also in the same living area (a separate room but under the same roof), with large windows so we could now see the privates 24 hours a day.

Mess and Maintenance week was the Marine Corps way of giving the recruits a vacation from recruit training. Basically the platoon was divided into groups of working parties then allocated out to the various sections at Edson Range to perform whatever tasks might be assigned. These tasks could be from cutting grass, repairing targets to Mess duty helping serve the meals and washing the endless trays and pots and pans. This would be the first time that we did not have direct supervision over our recruits. They left us in the morning and reported to whatever job assignments had been given to them. We had mixed feelings about Mess and Maintenance week, although we also had a break from the recruits we really hated to give up our charges to the supervision of other Marines, at least not at this stage of their training. But this started the subtle process of weaning the recruits away from us and vice versa, it also served as a slight introduction to what life would be like in the regular Marine Corps after their graduation. But mainly we felt that it gave the recruits the opportunity to become as loose as shit going through a goose, and would then have to be reminded they were still recruits and lower than whale shit!

The first day at Edson Range had gone smoothly and our series had been moved into the barracks, we were now ready for our week of Mess and Maintenance. The boss as usual had left his "Things to do List" for the upcoming week. Since the recruits would be gone during the day on their duty assignments. This would become our time for recruit evaluations. At the beginning of training we had the Secretary establish a file of 5X8 cards, one for every private. Each card contained the personal data of the recruit, his home of record, service number and a brief history taken form the recruit during the Boss's earlier briefing of the privates. It also contained the scores achieved during the various exams taken, more importantly it contained any comments we had made on the recruits performance to date. The recruits had been told that any information placed in this card would also be transferred to their permanent service record book and would follow them throughout their military career. This was partially true, naturally any recruit that was so screwed up that we thought might not make it, had to have each and every instance of poor performance documented, giving our superiors a day by day and a event by event history of these shit heads. In most cases the cards merely contained the standard entry of this Private is progressing satisfactorily through recruit training and is responding well to the adjustment of military life. If the recruit had been placed in a position of responsibility such as Guide, Squad Leader or House Mouse, etc . . .This was also annotated on the card. Since we had purposely told the privates about this file, we at times used it to our advantage. If a recruit had been called to the duty hut for screwing up we would give him a choice. "Look Fuck Stick, you just can't seem to get your head and ass wired. So we will just continue to put comments in your little card. Indicating that you are just one worthless piece of shit" or "I have a little drill that will probably help you get your head out of your ass" If you choose the drill, no comments will placed in your official card, "What will it be Sweetie"? Normally the private would of course choose the little drill, this drill could be anything from a quick choke, to an extended pit call. Oddly enough, regardless of the amount of comments made in the card. It did not seem to correct any behavior problems. at least not as well as the Drill.

Yeah! Mess and Maintenance was a time for us to get our paperwork in order, it also gave us the chance to try and further motivate any privates that seem to continue to have problems. We would make arrangements to have a recruit or recruits stay back from a work detail, so we could dedicate some one on one time to these sweethearts. I personally enjoyed these one on one sessions it allowed us to get a better insight to the recruit and our experience had taught us that these one on one sessions worked wonders in recruit motivation.

We attempted to throw the recruit off guard during this one on one time, and these sessions were certainly better than a pit call for the whole platoon just because one individual was not able to get his shit together. Maybe I would call for a certain recruit to report to me after morning chow. Naturally he would be wondering what the hell this crazy man wanted. More than likely he had been the recipient of many such duty hut encounters or at least a lot of yelling directed at him. Unlike past experiences, this would be a time where the rest of the platoon was not in the immediate area, and for all intents & purposes just the recruit and the D.I. would be present. The Duty Hut was staged for just such sessions, with a desk and a chair for the recruit. This in itself was unusual, the recruits were always at the position of attention when speaking to their D.I's. I would be sitting in the Hut waiting for the standard three knocks, followed by "Sir! Private . . .requests permission to enter the Duty Hut", "Screaming out" "Enter!" the recruit would enter and report to me as ordered. "Sooo Private . . .Why do you think you were called to my little place of heaven?" "Sir the Private does not know!" Was usually the standard answer, now the Private was expecting all hell to break loose, with whomever or me just going off on him with our machine gun like verbal barbs and terms of endearment. But now he was greeted with "Have a seat Private, make yourself comfortable. Sit down private. Maybe you would like a cup of coffee or maybe a cigarette. Secretary, get Private . . .a cup of coffee," "Aye Aye Sir," "Bullshit I will get it myself." By this time recruits normally fell into two categories those that were about ready to go into shock wondering why they were being treated so nicely and the other shit-heads who actually would kick back with the cup of coffee and maybe even a smoke. "Now private the reason I called you in here is because I have been going over your 5X8 card and it seems that you keep having problems, Why is that?" Many different answers would come from this question but all seemed to boil down to the same old shit. "Sir the Private is having problems adjusting to the stress of military life." "Well, you know Private, I can understand your problem and I can truly appreciate the dilemma that you're in and I really want to help you! You do believe that, don't you?" "Sir, Yes Sir" and you know why I want to help you don't you? It's because if you continue on this path, you won't, repeat, you won't make it to graduate or worse if you keep your mediocre ways and this half-assed attitude of yours, you will probably get some Marine killed. We depend on each other," at this point I would be speaking very softly and in a conversational sort of way, But now I would leap out of my chair and would be about two inches from the Privates face. This sudden change from a Dr. Jekyll to a Mr. Hyde always served its intended purpose of throwing the recruit even more off guard. Now Yelling, "You scummy piece of Shit, you had better knock off your cheap shit and get with the program. I will not allow you to wear my Marine Corps Emblem nor be called a Marine. You see, to many good men have died wearing our emblem and I would not want to disgrace their memory by letting some scum bag wear the same Emblem or hold the title of Marine just because I feel sorry for him. You have to work very hard to join our ranks, and I will help you, but only if you want to be helped. If you don't care than neither do I! For once in your miserable life you have the opportunity to set a goal and accomplish it. I believe you have never accomplished a damn thing, but now you can! and for the rest of your life say I was a United States Marine and no matter what, not anyone can take that away from you! Even those Shit for Brains, civilians know it is not easy to become a Marine, being a Marine sets you apart from all others. If it were fucking easy than the name Marine would mean nothing. OK, son it's your call, what will it be? No, don't tell me! the words don't mean shit, you must show me by your actions. Don't just talk the talk I want you to Walk the Walk. We will be keeping an eye on you. If you don't get your head and ass wired together, you are otta here, Yes otta here as a failure, able to go home to Mommy and tell her that you just didn't have the balls to hack it here, she might just as well have had a daughter." Now shouting even louder, "Get The Hell out of my Duty Hut, Move you worthless turd!"

Normally these one on one sessions had a dramatic effect, the changes in the recruit seemed to be immediate and dramatic. This scenario was being played out in all of the other Duty Huts in our series, all of us making a concerted effort to get through to those Privates that needed this extra helping hand. On many occasions the Series Gunnery Sergeant or even the Series Officer would sit in on our little talks with these recruits. Their presence just seemed to help our cause. You see the recruits believed that with the awesome power we as D.I.'s had as mere Sergeants or Staff Sergeants any rank higher than ours must have the power of the Almighty himself. This was as it should be, we stressed that even if the recruits had the right to speak to anyone in their chain of command or request mast as we called it, that the Corps whole being was based on a rank structure that should be used. The Series Gunnery Sergeant, Series Officer had a hell of a lot of other things to do than to listen to cry baby bullshit from a recruit.

Now understand there had to be a fine line drawn, because as Marines we knew the importance of the request mast procedure, yet how very important it was to use the chain of command. We emphasized to the recruits that while the opportunity was there. It had best be a problem that when taken by them up the chain of command up to and including the Commander in Chief (President of the United States) it best not have been a problem that could have been solved in the lower echelon of the rank structure. By the same token, God help that individual in the Chain of Command that did nothing to resolve a legitimate issue by a recruit or Marine. We believed that who ever did not attempt to resolve the problems of their men, probably had no right to be in the position of leadership. Everything in our Corps had a checks and balance system built into the regulations with most problems resolved by the maxim of Looking out for your men and their welfare. Believing in one another and the belief that all Marines regardless of rank looked out for each other created that bond we were trying to instill in our recruits.

The week of Mess and Maintenance had gone by very quickly and now it was time to get down for the real purpose of our being at Edson Range. It was now time for our recruits to become the master of their weapons, and learn the art of Marksmanship.

Even if Mess and Maintenance week had been a break for us, giving us the opportunity to get our paperwork together and 5 X 8 cards squared away with the required entries, we were ready and looking forward to getting started with the training cycle once again. Even the pranks we played on one another seemed to be wearing thin. Mess and Maintenance gave us a little more time on our hands than we had during the actual training time with our recruits, and we were no different than any other Marine with time on his hands. We occupied our time with the age-old art of playing pranks on one another or fucking with each other, to put it bluntly. We all knew that we must be on constant guard for any and everything! Hell one morning I awoke to find my damn car in the middle of the Squad Bay covered with shit paper. I knew for sure that Tagleri and Morse had something to do with this, but naturally they did not own up to a damn thing. The recruits all wide-eyed and trying desperately not to smile did not divulge any information as to the masterminds of this incident.

I of course had to try and avenge myself and told our Secretary a recruit who resembled the legendary Icabod Crane from the legend of Sleepy Hollow, You know glasses, beak nose and all arms and legs, that we would help Sgt. Morse clean his car. Well Morse had this old blue piece of shit Dodge Chrysler, but he loved that car dearly, anyway he would not let anyone touch that piece of shit. I took his keys without his knowledge one day before he was about to shove off, and told the Secretary to fill the back with shaving cream, because Sgt Morse believed it helped the interior of his car? Now understand a recruit would not question any method, after all we were all crazy men anyway, well Morse is about to leave and steps outside the barracks to see his car, driven by our Secretary, pulling up front with fucking shaving cream just pouring out of the back seat. Oh shit, you should have seen the look on his face. Damn it was great! now of course all the other Hats were in on what was about to happen and all had the chance to see Morse just go out of his mind.

"What the fuck did you do to my car, Oh shit my Car!" Yeah we were ready to get back to training and so were the recruits. Naturally the Secretary caught Holy Hell for the shaving cream, but you could tell he enjoyed the joke as much as we did.

The next week of training was called "snapping-in-week," the recruits would learn the different positions from which they would be firing their weapons, Off hand, Kneeling, Sitting and Prone Positions. They would spend all day for the next week getting in and out of those positions, with instructions on how to aim at a target, and hearing all the commands they would hear when firing on the rifle range. They would aim in on a barrel with targets painted on it, this allowed the recruits to practice getting in and out of each position from which they would fire. It helped not only to get accustomed to the positions but also to familiarize themselves with the commands they would hear before they started a live string of fire. Anyone who has had to qualify on a Marine Corps Rifle Range, understands the need to practice and as we called it Snapping In. You find muscles that you never thought you had. We practiced getting in and out of positions, proper placement of a rifle sling on your arm, adjusting your position so that it became rock solid. The more solid the position the better to hit the target, and with the Marine Corps reputation for marksmanship, we left nothing to chance, from how a target should look through the sight of your weapon, to the proper breathing technique, and trigger squeeze before firing one round down range! The recruits practiced and practiced until like everything else even this would become second nature.

As with all other instruction the Marine Corps had acronyms to help you remember and the range was no different. BRASS was heard throughout the range. Breathe, Relax, Aim in, Slack (Slack taken in on trigger), Squeeze, POW ! BULLS EYE! As always our job was to maintain discipline, provide instructions and assist the Marksmanship instructors in their efforts to teach the privates the fine points of shooting more importantly hitting your target. Snapping in was a boring but necessary evil. We knew that for the recruits snapping in was probably as exciting as their class on the importance of buying Savings Bonds. Snapping in week always seemed to be a very long , mainly because our assistance during this stage of training was to ensure that the recruits got into the proper firing positions, and always checking for what we called unsafe weapons. On the rifle range all weapons must be considered to be safe weapons, this is a rifle with its bolt locked to the rear, weapon safety on and naturally no rifle magazine in the weapon. This sounds easy but as always we had a few shitheads who would forget to lock their bolt to the rear or whatever. The importance of a safe weapon could not be over stressed because the recruits would be handling live ammo in the following week and if they did not learn it now, they might just shoot themselves or someone else.

"Oh No, No!" I yelled as I inspected the weapons in the snapping in circle, the recruits would leave their weapons in the snapping in circle while they attended classes on proper firing positions and techniques of firing, seated in the bleachers at each location. "Who has rifle number 242096, I said who had rifle number 242096?"

"Sir, that is the private's rifle number," answered one of the recruits. "Not you again, this is the second time I have found your weapon unsafe, I know it wasn't your fault, Right, the fucking weapon had a mind of its own, is that right?" "Sir, Yes Sir!" "Bullshit! you can now join the rest of those turds that have miracle weapons. You maggots have been told time and time again what a safe weapon is! Now I guess we will do bends and thrusts till I get tired. Ready exercise, I can't hear you! Louder, I want all of Edson Range to hear you, I said Louder!" These little exercise routines had the effect we wanted. Normally on the first day you would find a number of unsafe weapons in the circle, but after a few exercises this number would be down to nothing as the recruits learned the extreme importance of an unsafe weapon and its consequences.

The great thing about the range is that we finally got away from the constant noise of those damn planes at San Diego's Airport. We were now surrounded by the hills of Camp Pendleton to the east and the Pacific Ocean to our West. This was certainly more conducive to a Marine-training environment than the Depot. The sounds now came from the ranges, a constant barrage of rifle fire as the ranges operated and recruits practiced what they were learning in snapping in week. You could hear the commands of the Range, "All ready on the right, All ready on the left, this will be one string of rapid fire, Watch your Targets, Targets!"

In the evening it was not unusual to see the night skies lit up with flares, and a string or two of red tracers as the Marines underwent their Infantry Training on the surrounding hillsides. All of this served to add a bit more credence to the martial world the recruits were now becoming a part of and the possibility of their going to War seemed to finally start sinking in. The range was the mid-point of the training cycle and more importantly, the recruits were now undergoing that part of their training that was synonymous with the name Marine, how to shoot their weapon. Every Marine must qualify with his weapon, and once that first round left his weapon down range, most would start understanding that all the training they had received or would receive was not a game. This job could really be life or death!

"OK you bunch of killers, you have exactly 3 minutes to get your asses in the barracks, stow your gear, make a head call and get in the classroom. Well, Go!" "Aye Aye Sir!" the routine now very well established, the House Mouse had my three footlockers placed at the head of the squad bay, pack of Salems in the left corner, cup of coffee with 99 grains of sugar so all was as it should be.

Classroom time now becoming what it was intended to be, going over the days events and the items and events for the up-coming day or days. Mail Call, followed by showers and hygiene inspection. Classroom time now became a very important ques-tion and answer period for the recruits. Naturally all questions were preceded by "Sir Private . . .Requests permission to speak to the Drill Instructor." "What the fuck you want turd?" The recruits were comfortable with the procedures on how to do things, and everyday led to more and more questions.

We at this point were fast becoming what we were sup-posed to be to these young men. Their teachers! Unlike any teachers in any school they had ever attended but teachers none-the-less. They were finally beginning to understand the rela-tionship and became more open in their questions. They knew we would not tolerate any infraction of the procedures they had been taught, however they now were willing to take a chance and ask more questions on just about everything you could imagine. Most of the questions fell into the category of what the Marine Corps was like and what it was they could expect when (and we told them if) they graduated. Sometimes some shithead would actually want to know what we did in our off duty time away from them. Our standard answer was to read the Marine Corps GuideBook, so we could fuck with them even more than we did now. Even if they smiled at this response, I honestly felt they believed this shit, after all we still were those crazy bastards let loose from some insane asylum.

The other Hats and myself tolerated these type of questions and we all admitted that we really started to enjoy the classroom sessions at this stage of training because we now started to inject many of the Corps ideals, traditions, and philosophy into our sessions. "A Marine and his weapon is the most feared adversary on the face of the earth. We have never been first to leave a battlefield and you jerk offs better understand one damn thing, the public expects that on a battlefield we will be nothing less than animals, but in any other environment we are always expected to be gentleman. We have a tradition that no other military service has. That's why, ladies, the doggies (Army) don't teach History because they have none. We are the Eagle, Globe and Anchor! We took the Eagle from the Air Force, the Anchor, from the Navy and on the seventh day God Rested and we took the World. If you graduate you had better walk with your heads held high, people know what it took for you to become a Marine, many have tried to claim our title but few actually make it. That why a Marine always takes care of his fellow Marines. We are the few and damn it, the very fucking Proud! Is that Understood?" "Sir, Yes Sir!" "I don't hear shit! Is That Understood!" "Sir, Yes Sir!"

Like I said, training recruits was much like training a boxer for a fight, the Corps placed a great deal of emphasis on the recruits being able to qualify with their weapons. The range always seemed to require a different type of motivational approach, we knew we must keep the privates at their prime, yet we also knew that the tension must not become so intolerable that the shitheads psych themselves out, before they even fired their weapons. Each day of firing would give them and us instant results, whether or not they had achieved a passing score to qualify with their rifles.

We had different methods of letting the recruits release their pent up frustrations, one such tool was the use of the Hog Board. We had told the recruits before arriving at Edson Range that they should ask girlfriends, Moms, wives or who ever, to send photos for entry into the platoons beauty pageant. We of course asked that the pictures be as revealing as possible, but most would just be plain High School photos. A photo received was then placed as an entry on the Platoons Hog Board. Voting would take place on the day before qualification. Once the photos started coming in,

Mail Call also became a good tension reliever. We could feel the photos inside the letters of the recruits as we passed out each letter. As usual we would call out the name of the recruit and give him his letter. "Pvt Jones," "Sir Pvt. Jones", "Jones! What did I tell all you maggots about any shit written on the outside of any letters." "Sir! Nothing was to be written on the outside of the letter other than Privates address and Name Sir!" "Then what the hell is this shit? A plain white fucking envelope is all I fucking asked for and now I see all this civilian bullshit! Sealed with a Kiss or I love you, I miss you and all kinds of other horse shit. Sealed with a Kiss my ass Jones. Put the letter on the deck and she wants it sealed with a kiss, you will do it! As you are doing pushups you will kiss your damn letter." "Aye Aye Sir!" This type of harassment continued with each letter or package. I could tell that the platoon always got a big kick out of this stuff and kept them motivated. "Oh No No, Pizza Face you got a letter, I do believe it has a photo, Here you go! Damn it smells like a WhoreHouse anyway. Open it up! Hey you do have a photo! Is that your girlfriend? No way, you paid some gal to send you a photo", "Sir No Sir." "I can't believe any Hog would like your dumb ass, especially one as good looking as this one. Well! put it on the board, Son!" Like I said, the recruits just ate this stuff up. Mind you, never any lack of discipline on their parts, but somehow a bonding now seemed to be forming between the recruits and us, it was a bond of brotherhood that all Marines seemed to share. We knew that the recruits had started this bonding process with one another, a shared kinship based on their hardship (Boot Camp and Us).

Time, as always was very important to us, we tried many techniques to help teach the recruits the importance of any training they had received. One of my favorites at the range was to tape a flashlight on the stock of a weapon and turn all the lights out and the flashlight (Penlight) on. We had been telling the turds that the slightest movement could throw the round (bullet) off it's target. I would show them with the help of this light how even improper breathing could move the weapon, the light would move up and down to my breathing rhythm, jerk the trigger and the light moves up and right. The recruits now had a visual of the effects of not applying the proper shooting techniques they were being taught. "Remember you bunch of Killers, you can shoot all you want but it's only the Hits that count! You had better be a better shot than the person you're shooting at, or you will be dead!"

"BRASS, Breath in, relax, aim in, gently take up the slack on the trigger, squeeze the trigger and I do mean squeeze, some of you might know how to squeeze, you know like gently squeezing a set of tits. Squeeze,do not, repeat not, jerk the damn trigger, then POW Bull Eye. Right!" "Sir, Yes Sir!"

"OK sweeties in 30 minutes you will be hitting the racks, Guide!" "Sir!" "They have 15 minutes to shit, shower and shave, 15 minutes of bullshit time, you know the drill, 1st and 2nd squad in the showers, while 3rd and 4th shave and shit. Do It!" "Aye Aye Sir!" Exactly 30 minutes later, 3 knocks sounded on the Duty Hut hatch, "Sir, Guide Requests Permission to enter the Duty Hut." "Enter! What do you want Guide?" "Sir, the platoon is ready for hygiene inspection." As I left the Hut the platoon was formed and ready for hygiene inspection, another nightly routine down to a fine science by the platoon. Inspection over it was now time for the privates to hit the rack. "OK sweeties its night, night time, prepare to mount, Mount!, One, Two, the recruits now in their racks lying at the position of attention. OK you killers, we will now practice our facing movements. This was another game the recruits actually seemed to enjoy, if you gave a platoon more than three facing movements in one direction, the third command made the turds fall right out of the racks. Left Face! Left Face! Left Face!, Holy shit! Pizza Face and Lard Ass actually bounced on that last facing movement." "GOODNIGHT Sweeties," "GOODNIGHT SIR"! The recruits now learned to differentiate between this type of harassment and let's say a good old fashion pit call. They actually seemed to enjoy this game of facing movements, it served to put them in the rack happy and surely eased the tensions of the day.

They knew that the morning would bring them to their first real live fire with their weapons. Tensions among the privates would be at an all time high during firing week, they knew the emphasis that both the Corps and we placed on the ability to shoot and hit your target. You see, you weren't shit unless you were able to qualify with your weapon. So our harassment was also away for the recruits to ease this mounting tension, and I believe they knew what we were attempting to do and enjoyed this type of harassment.

"Fire Watch!" "Sir, Fire Watch!" "I will be in the next squad bay, visiting Plt. Cmdr. Ssgt Mimiaga I best not hear any bullshit or horseplay from the platoon. If I do your ass is grass and I will be the lawn mower." "Aye Aye Sir!" With the recruits in the rack and all my paperwork for the day finished, it was time to shoot the breeze with the other hats on duty. Of course our usual theme would be how much better each of our platoons was than the other. Mixed in with the standard bullshit of trying to out fox one another. Ssgt Mimiaga's hut was our normal gathering place for these sessions, it was not unusual for not only the Duty D.I.s to be there, but on some occasions even the Series Gunns would join us. "Platoon Attention!" screamed Mimiaga's Firewatch as I entered the Squad Bay, "Shut the Fuck Up! What's a matter with you? Your platoon's already asleep, and you damn well know the other D.I.s in the series will be here to visit your Plt. Cmdr. Right?" "Sir, the Private has been instructed to Sound Attention whenever anyone other than the Privates Drill Instructors or Plt Cmdr enter the Squad Bay after lights out." "Yeah that's right, Firewatch you do just like I told you to do!" yells Ssgt Mimiaga from inside his Duty Hut. "Ok Firewatch, carry on!" I knew that this was the drill. Sounding attention not only served to get the turds used to proper military etiquette. When they finally entered the Marine Corps, but is served as an alarm to any Hat on duty, you know in case we were giving a little choke or two to some turd that screwed up during the day. "Hey Ssgt Mimiaga how's it going?" "Hernandez, just give me a damn smoke, want some coffee?" "Yeah sure! but shit another smoke? I don't know why I visit you, and damn your always bumming smokes from me." "You visit me cause you think might learn my secret of taking 1st on the range, that's why." "Bullshit, my turds, as always, will be the number one platoon." "My ass," says Tagleri as he walks in and pours himself a cup of Joe. "You can't possibly be talking about who will be number one herd on the range." "Oh shit now it was Perez's turn to start his cheap shit. "Sammy you have never had a herd that took first in anything except maybe buying fucking savings bonds." "You're talking out your ass, because I just a little while ago, was showing my turds my own special technique on how to fire a weapon." "What! you couldn't hit your ass with both hands!" "Yeah, Yeah! just wait and see." "Hey who's playing chess with me tonight asks Mimiaga." "Not me, after I have my coffee I'm going straight to hit the rack, I need my beauty sleep." "Yeah, for the next hundred years, with that mug of yours." "Screw You Tag" "Hernandez what the hell happened the other day at the snapping in circle?" "Don't know what you're talking about." "I saw your Boss running out of the target shack, chasing a damn truck." I started laughing to the point of almost shitting my drawers. "No Shit! Damn and the Boss thought he got away with it." "What the hell are you talking about?" "You know how the Boss, has a thing for dippsty dumpsters, well he got pissed at the Squad Leaders and the Guide, seems they had screwed up something he told them to do. So he calls them out of the snapping in circle, left the rest of the herd with me, anyway he tells them they were so Fucked Up that he was going to Shit Can the whole lot of them. So, he puts them in the dumpster, tells them he had better not hear one sound from any of them. He goes to the target shed to get a cup of java, so that the recruits can think about the error of their ways. In the meantime the damn truck comes to load up the dumpster and take it to the dump. The driver pulls up and loads the dumpster on his truck, with our turds still inside!" "No Shit!" "Yeah but it gets better, naturally the recruits don't make a sound, the Boss comes out of the target shed and sees the truck pull away with the dumpster full of our sweethearts. He starts running after the truck, yelling for the driver to stop! Now Get this shit, the driver finally stops and the Boss tells him the whole story. But the driver is some old retired Gunny and tells the Boss if he wants the turds back, it will cost him $40 bucks. Boss says Bullshit, $40 big ones, no way in hell. Driver says it ain't no skin off his ass if the recruits end up at the dump. But he starts to feel sorry for the Boss and lets him go for only $20. Can you believe that! Man our ass would have been grass if he had gone out the gate with our turds. Holy Shit, for sure your tired asses would be in the brig."

"Hell, remember what happen with the last herd we had here, Morse ends up choking some young Marine Private First Class, he had the recruits down in the butts, pulling target detail. We didn't know that the range had Marines firing for their annual qualification on the group of targets next to ours, naturally they were pulling their own targets, well Morse is checking on his turds and spots this one fast asleep down by the target shed. He goes ape shit, thinks it's a recruit and reaches down and starts to choke the dog shit out of him. This guy starts to fight back which of course just makes Morse even angrier. Then Morse spots the PFC chevron (rank insignia) on the front of this guys cover, he immediately lets go of this guy, realized he is a Marine and that he has really screwed up. What to do, so without batting an eye he commences to tell this young PFC. "Look Marine, I know you learned better in boot camp about sleeping on duty. And that little choke is for all the shit you thought you got away with, Now I want you to carry on with your duties, Understand?" Morse starts to walk away praying that this turd doesn't report his dumb ass, when this Marine jumps up and says "Aye Aye Sir!" "Now can you believe that shit?" "Fucking turd probably needed a good choke any damn way" says Tag. We all just shook our heads in agreement. "Well, guess I'll go and finally hit the rack, you know the first morning of firing is always a bitch. With us having to get half the herd down in the butts while the other half is on the firing line, getting our target assignments, and all the other stuff that needs to get done before the first goat can actually get on the firing line." "I heard the LT is thinking about a little forced march after qualification day," "No Shit!" "Ah Roo Ah," yells Tag, "I love that kind of shit." "Yeah, I thought you would, but we just have to wait for the official word." "Man that's hot stuff!" We all just had to chime in with a big "Fuck You Tag!" " Damn Grunts were all alike, if you can't think of anything to do, then how about we just go for a little 20 mile march."

Here we go Again! Firing day had finally arrived, now came a solid four days of shooting with the fifth day being qualification day for the herd. This was a week where all of us had to be present. The two D.I.s' and the Plt Cmdr's from each platoon. The platoon would be split up with two squads down in the butts. The other squads on the firing line, they would then rotate. The detail in the butts job was to pull the targets up and down, score and mark each hit, while the other two squads were shooting on the firing line. Marking and, as we called, discing the targets, was a job in itself. It required that when a recruit on the firing line shot on his target, the recruit down in the butts pulled the target down and places a spotter (small disc) on the target. Run the target back up in the air, so the shooter could see where his shot was on the target. The butt puller then scored the shot. A method in which he would use a long pole with a large colored metal disc attached at one end. The color of the disc depicting the score the shooter had received. This allowed the shooter not only to see his point, but also because of the spotter on the target see where he shot. Now if the dipshit saw that there was no spotter and then he saw the disc wave from left to right in front of the target, well, we called it a "Maggies drawers" or a fucking complete miss on the whole big-ass target.

The privates had not only been taught the proper firing positions but had also learned to make DOPE changes. This was a method for correction of either windage or elevation to the sights of the weapon, which would change the strike of the round (bullet) on the target. Let's say a recruit shot three times and the rounds struck the lower left of the target. The shooter by adjusting the sights for windage or elevation could move the strike of the round to the bullseye. This was the ideal situation because the shooter in this case was firing in a consistent manner and hitting in the same area for each shot. Now if this turd shot three times and the hits were all over the damn place, then there was no way to adjust the strike of the bullet. This was because this dip did not have proper sight alignment or proper sight picture (what he saw through the sights), or had an inconsistent position. Naturally good butt service had a lot to do with the ability to make dope changes, if you had some maggot that screwed things up down in the butts, then the shooter had no idea of what the hell was happening. Butt detail wasn't rocket science, but if a recruit can screw something up, then he damn sure would! All of this required constant contact between the firing line and the butts. The Range Personnel would be up on the firing line in a moveable tower. A Marine from the Range, had constant contact with the butts by a field telephone, this tower could be moved to each of the distances the recruit was require to shoot from, 200 yds, 300 yds, and 500 yd. line. His contact down in the butts was another Marine located in the Sound Shed. This Marine would parrot the orders being given to the recruits on the firing line and tell the butt detail when to run the targets up and down, by use of a PA system, it was a marvel to watch this coordinated effort.

"OK Killers, all commands in the butts will come from the Sound Shed! We will do some practice commands, these commands will come over the PA system and the commands are not any you have not already heard in the snapping in circle. If you screw up while pulling the targets, the Marine in the Sound Shed will be notified by the center of the firing line and then, Sweeties I will be told, and I will be on you like stink on shit, is that Understood?" " Sir, Yes Sir!" The target you have been assigned to pull is the same target you will be shooting on when it is your turn to go to the firing line. If you give poor butt service to your fellow recruit, then I'm sure you will receive the same type of service. Turn to on your target assignments! "Aye Aye Sir!"

Each platoon was assigned a group of 25 targets, all commands were given from the center of the line, for each string of fire and each relay of fire. Since the privates would be shooting from distances of 200, 300 and 500 yds, each yard line had different positions from which the recruit would fire from and even different types of fire, slow and rapid. Slow fire meant the private would fire one round, the target would be pulled down, scored and marked, the shooter would see where he had shot, shoot another round and attempt to hit the bullseye and or make a DOPE change. Rapid fire meant the shooter sees the targets come up in the air, gets in position starts shooting as fast as he can squeeze the trigger (Semi Automatic Fire) and shoots as many rounds that have been designated for that string of fire. Only after the designated time frame will the targets be pulled down and scored. For the first four days the turds would be shooting double strings of rapid fire, this allowed them to make dope changes and try and get all of their rounds in the bullseye. But once they shot for qualification the dope changes they had made during the week for rapid fire had better be right on, no second chance was given on qual. day. All of the firing was an attempt to try and simulate what types of fire they might have to do in the real thing. In combat they might be able to see and pick their targets (Slow Fire) or maybe lay down a massive volume of fire (Rapid Fire), in either case you could shoot all you want, but if you don't hit what you shoot at, than it don't mean shit!

"All ready on the left, all ready on the right, Shooter's this will be your first string of slow fire. Watch your targets, when your targets appear you may commence firing." We were down in the butts and could hear the commands from the firing line. Now would come the commands from the sound shed. "On my command, palms up, you will push your targets all the way up in the air, Targets!" Now all the targets were run up in the air by the privates. We could now hear the sound of the shots as the shooters commenced their first string of fire. The job of the butts was to watch the impact area. Which was about 20 yards behind the targets, a pit of sand that when a round was fired on the firing line you could see the impact of the bullet, this meant the target had been fired upon and you then scored and marked the target. We of course were below the firing line and in a safe area from the impact of the rounds.

"What the hell are you doing? You blind or what? Didn't you see the impact of that round? Well, pull the target down and mark it, You Dipshit!" All the Hats assigned to the butt detail were now all over the butts, "You mark that damn target, Slow Butt service target 24 was heard from the sound shed, Damn one of my turds." "You, target 24, get your shit together or I will have you in the fucking impact area!" As always we were everywhere, this was great, the air was filled with the sounds of rifle fire, commands from both the line and the shed, and like I said we were everywhere. "You, Pizza face, what the hell is the problem? You best get your head out of your ass, pull that target down and score it. That's a bullseye not a four, Zit juice must have crept in you brain. You have your shit together?" "Sir, Yes Sir!" We knew it would take at least one day before the recruits got their act together, but nothing done incorrectly was ever tolerated by the Hats.

On the firing line the Boss and Morse and the rest of the members of our series would be going crazy! They would be going up and down the line checking each recruit, to ensure that they were following all instructions from the center of the line. The firing line on the first day would appear to be an organized mass of chaos. Not only did the recruits have the Plt. Cmdr. and Sgt Morse to contend with, they would also have their marksmanship instructor and the rifle coaches to help them. The Corps left nothing to chance when it came to firing our weapons. A rifle coach was assigned to every five targets being fired upon. When we rotated the butt detail assignment, Sgt Morse would bring the 1st and 2nd squads into the butts after their string of fire and I would go to the firing line with the 3rd and 4th squads. The Plt Cmdr always remained on the firing line. To add emphasis to the importance of this stage of training, the Series Gunns and the Series Officer would also be on the firing line for the entire week.

"Squad Leaders!" "Sir, Squad Leaders reporting as ordered Sir!" "Take your squads and march them to the two hundred yard line, I will meet you there, the Plt Cmdr is already waiting for your squads. Do it!" "Aye Aye Sir!" I could now see the 1st and 2nd squads entering the butts, "Sir 1st and 2nd squads reporting to the Drill Instructor." "Drill Instructor, Sgt. Morse will be here shortly, have your squads go to their assigned targets, which would be the same targets you fired on this morning. Move it!" "Aye Aye Sir!" Morse was now down in the butts, "Well, how did they do?" "Same old shit, some of them shoot better than Wyatt Earp, others couldn't hit their ass with both hands. The Boss says to do our nightly ritual with those shit heads that screwed up." "Well Alright and Hot Damn, it would be a good night! See you back at the Hut!" As I approached the 200-yard line I could see the Boss with our squads, they were down on one knee. "You already know, ladies, that all commands will come from the center of the line, none of the commands will be new to you. Make sure all weapons are safe weapons, listen to your coaches, practice your BRASS, remember proper sight alignment, sight picture and maintain a good solid shooting position, do all of this and POW, I want and will see nothing but bulls eyes, Right!" "Sir, Yes Sir!" "Let's fucking do it, Rock and Roll!"

"Hey Boss, what's up?" "I damn sure hope these turds do better than the first two squads, watch them close, we had a few that forgot all about trigger squeeze and dope changes. They were jerking the trigger, shooting all over the damn targets. The L.T. says he wants to make sure all the recruits qualify. He's a good Officer, been helping out where he can and lets us do our thing. The Series Gunns must miss his D.I. days cause he's been up and down the line adding inspiration." "I sure as hell knew what the Boss meant by this, the Gunny had a way of instilling fear, yet at the same time motivating the privates. Shit! he did the same with us, we often thought that if we screwed up real bad, the Gunns, was not above giving us a choke or two. The L.T. and he made a great team. With the L.T's quiet no bullshit demeanor and the Gunnys

I'll kick you in the ass, if you don't do your job attitude, let us know that we had their support and also let us know to stand by if we screwed up.

We all knew that today would bring a whole rash of fuck ups, the first day of firing always did, and as always we would be around to correct the screw ups. Up and down the line we went, OH NO! What the Hell you doing? How do you expect to make dope changes? Look at your target your shooting all over the damn place. Sure looks like you're jerking the trigger, I told you squeeze the trigger. Put your finger in your mouth, No shithead not the whole damn finger! Just the tip, now bite down on it, I said bite! Hurts, Right? Good! You will see that the finger is a little sensitive, now go up on the line and try shooting again. POW, See! you got a damn bullseye! Don't smile at me, Asshole! Just keep putting them in the black! You over there on target 35, how the hell did you miss that whole big ass target?" "Sir, the Private doesn't know Sir!" Bullshit! A whole week on the snapping in circle, and you still don't know? Get down in you firing position. Now, crank off a round. No! No! Your position is as loose as shit going through a goose, do it again but this time I want the sling tighter, and your position like a rock. Now you have a good tight position. You got good sight alignment, sight picture?" "Sir, Yes Sir!" "Close your eyes, now open them, do you still have the same sight picture, "Sir, Yes Sir!" Your problem was a loose position you should always have the same sight picture. Now try the procedure all over again! Still the same? OK! When your ready crank off a round POW, Son you are about two inches left from the bullseye at 9 O'clock. Go two clicks right, POW, WOW dead center on the black, a fucking bulls eye! "Thank You Sir!" "Look, shithead don't thank me, the United States Government thanks me, twice a month on payday, you just keep shooting that way." "Aye Aye Sir!"

All day for the next four days we would be going up and down the line, coaxing, belittling, yelling doing our best to get these young men to shoot. Each day would also see the recruits get more proficient, but for now this first day was finally drawing to an end.

The day of firing finally over and all our squads back together forming our platoon.

"Fall In!" At this command the recruits finished what they were doing and rushed to get in a platoon formation. "Count Guide!" "Sir. Count Guide," the Plt Guide now counted each member of the platoon, letting us know that all our little chicks were back together. This counting of the platoon members had been done since our first day with the herd back in San Diego. This not only served to make sure we had all of our charges, but also placed the emphasis that we Marine's never ever left anyone behind.

We now had the scores for each of our privates from the days firing. Rifle scores were placed into four separate groups, Rifle Expert, Sharpshooter, Marksman and those that did not obtain enough of a score to qualify or UNQ's as we called them. The goal of course was that each recruit qualify, any person falling into the first three groups would then be allowed to wear the appropriate shooting badge on his uniform. This told the whole world how well you were able to shoot, by the same token, the absence of a shooting badge also told the whole world that you were a non-shooting puke, and who wants to go to War with a non-shooter.

"OK ladies!" yelled Sgt. Morse, "The following privates will fall out and come to the front of the platoon." As he sounded off a dozen names each recruit left the formation and now stood in front of the platoon. "Look at them! These dog breaths did not qualify with their weapons! You twelve will not, repeat not, march with the rest of the platoon. You will wear your covers backwards, so everyone can see and will know that you are a bunch of UNQ's. Now you UNQ's, Lay down, close your eyes, if you can't shoot, than you will probably be shot and then you will be just dead. Your inability to shoot will probably cause the death of others. So, for now let's pretend your dead, nothing matters anymore, all that you were or intended to be is gone. No goals to achieve, just nothing, you are now just chow for the worms. If this were real the next thing that would happen would be that someone would place one of your two dog tags between your teeth and kick your lower jaw shut, lodging them between your upper and lower teeth. That's so your love ones can identify and then claim your worthless asses." As the recruits lay on the ground with their eyes closed, I now placed a flower on each of them and had them fold their hands across their chest clutching the flower. "Yep, just plain fucking dead" I repeated, "Think about it! We will perform this little game after each firing day. And for the next three days, all you have to do to become part of this group is not qualify, and all you have to do to get out of this group is to shoot the way you have been taught to shoot. So the rest of you maggots watching your fellow recruits here on the ground, just screw up and you can join them as worm bait. As for you shit heads already on the ground, continue with your cheap shit, than this will one-day be the real thing. Get on your feet and form a separate UNQ squad. Do it!"

As we marched our platoon to the squad bays, the rest of the platoons in the series joined us, each with their own squad of UNQ's, marching behind the platoon, covers on backwards and heads hung down in shame. This embarrassment and classification was not over, tonight before the privates hit the rack, we would fallout in a series formation with all platoons present. Any recruit in the series that had sung in a choir or could sing would be placed at the entryway of the upper squad bay. From this point the choirboys could look down on the rest of the series. They would be dressed up in sheets like togas wrapped around them. The Series Gunns would then have all the non-quals march in front of the series and would then give a eulogy for those turds that failed to qualify. "Lord we have before you some non-shooting recruits, because of their inability to fire their weapons we know that you will call them very soon. We also know that if the Army or the Navy ever looked on Heaven Scenes. They will find the streets are guarded by United States Marines. Forgive them for not understanding sight alignment, sight picture, let their friends forgive them for being non-shooters. But Father we all know that the Corps can not forgive them for letting down their platoon, their Series and the Corps". The Gunny would say this in a very soft voice, with the choirboys singing Amazing Grace, and then ever so softly, hum the Marines Hymn. Oh it was great! Brought fucking tears to your eyes, Then the entire series prompted by us would bow their heads and ask that the non-quals be forgiven by some of the Corps legendary heroes'. "Forgive them Chesty Puller, Forgive them Dan Daily, Forgive them Col Edson., on and on We even had a small burial detail dig miniature graves in the sandy area below the pull up bars, in front of the squad bay for each of these turds. A nametag for each of the non-shooters placed very solemnly in the grave and then covered. Gunny would close with, "If you don't qualify, just remember this burial detail will probably end up being the real thing for you maggots. Sure it placed the non-quals in a very somber mood but it also added a lot of levity and helped release tension for those turds that did qualify on this their first day of firing. Experience had taught us that most of the recruits who now had grave markers, would qualify in the next couple of days and that their number would dwindle as the week came to an end. At this stage of training the recruits were beginning to understand the importance of not letting yourself down, and the extreme importance of not letting your platoon, series and ultimately your Corps and fellow Marines' down.

"Platoon Halt! Form for Chow!" "Sir, Form for Chow, Aye Aye Sir!" "Do It!" Like a precision machine. The recruits went through an intricate series of drill movements that would form the 4 squads into two single lines. This required the 2nd and 3rd squad to take one step forward then a step to the left or right. March in place for twenty steps, all members halting on the last step and then coming to the parade rest position, starting from the front of the lines until the last member in both lines was finally at parade rest. This was followed with the platoon sounding off with, War is our business and business is good, Ah Ooh Rah. It was a beautiful sight to behold. Just because we were at the Rifle Range did not mean drill movements were neglected, and when it came to forming for chow, each platoon tried to out do the other.

Another day had begun with last evening's eulogy by the Series Gunns, just a memory, but serving as a bleak reminder for any non-quals of the embarrassment they would suffer if they or anyone else failed to qualify. As usual after we put the herds to bed and finished our paperwork, we all met in Ssgt Mimiaga's' duty office for our nightly cup of Joe and to shoot the shit. Since rifle range duty required that all of us be present most of us would just stay at the Range rather then driving the distance back to Diego. Naturally the more present the more stories we had to tell. Even the Series Officer would on occasion join us. His comments normally limited too, asking us how we thought the training was progressing. What he could do to help and support us. He was a good Officer looking out for his men and their welfare. He never stayed very long allowing us to openly shoot the shit about the events of the day and the behavior and subsequent corrective measures we had found necessary to take on our recruits. He was not immune to our pranks and much to the Series Gunns' chagrin, we did various things to screw with the L.T. Just last night the Series Gunns' had chewed my ass out. We all knew when the L.T. was going to join us, the Gunny made sure of that. Anyway I had placed a recruit in each of two wall lockers, one recruit had a hot cup of black coffee, and the other had a cup of coffee with cream and sugar. After placing them in the wall lockers I gave them their instructions. The L. T. and the Gunny walked into the office. We came to attention. " Good Evening Sir," "Good evening Sergeant Hernandez," "Would the Lieutenant care for a cup of coffee?" The Gunny now gave me that what's up look. "Yes I would, replied the L.T.," "Black or cream and sugar Sir?" "Black Please." I walked over to the wall locker that had the recruit in it with the hot black coffee. I took a nickel out of my pocket and placed it through the upper slats of the wall locker. I opened the locker's door and the recruit stuck his right hand out with the black cup of coffee. "Sir Black coffee, Aye Aye Sir", says the private. The Gunny just goes ape shit! The L.T. accepts his coffee and starts to sip it, with a twinkle in his eye. "What the hell are you doing Hernandez!, get that turd out of here!" screams the Gunny. Naturally I chased the recruit out of the wall locker and duty hut, then I went over to the second wall locker and chased the second recruit out of his locker. The Gunny's eyes just bulge out, the L.T. finishes his cup and just says "Gentlemen have a good evening, Sgt Hernandez", "Yes Sir;" "Good cup of coffee! Now lets just see if we can get everyone to qualify by the end of the week." "Aye Aye Sir," we all chimed in. "Damn you Hernandez! I should put your ass in the pit! Damn it to hell, you all have to quit screwing with the Series Officer." The Gunny was only half-serious, he and the L.T. had established a good rapport, we knew how far we could go and how much the L.T. would tolerate. The Chain of Command was too much ingrained in us, to push the pranks too far. We knew that these pranks made the L.T. feel more in tune with us, but we never forgot for a minute that he was our Officer in Charge, and a damn good one!

We only had three days left of practice firing before actual qualification day, the pressure would be building up in the platoons as each day passed. Just because you qualified one day did not mean you would qualify on qualification day. Anything could happen, you might drop your weapon for example. That was a big fucking NO! NO!. Not only because it let the rest of the world know you were a dufus, but dropping your weapon could knock your sights loose and then you were really screwed. The privates had been taught very early in their training that you had better never ever drop your rifle. "Oh Shit, you maggot I can't believe you just dropped your rifle! That weapon is your life, it's like dropping your woman! For this little incident you maggot breath! Will sleep with it! Not just next to you, it will be broken down into its three main groups and you will sleep on top of it! Is that Understood?" After a night of sleeping on top of a rifle, very few weapons were dropped a second time.

Damn, I could not believe how fast the last three days had gone by. The recruits would be returning from evening chow, our little gravesites had dwindled to only six for the entire series. Two of the gravesites were from our platoon. Those two turds just could not seem to get their shit in one bag and qualify. They had come within 10 points today, closer to qualification then they had been in the last four days. We would have to keep a very close eye on those two tomorrow. Unlike the rest of the week, on qualification day it was all up to the recruits. They would make their own dope changes and we D.I.'s and the Plt. Cmdrs had to remain off the firing line. It would all be in the hands of the privates, their call all the way on qualification day.

"Boss! the platoon is back from chow and they have already shit and showered, Morse is just about finished with mail call and I have the Hog Board Detail! The classroom is ready to go Boss!"

Entering the classroom we saw two recruits in the corner of the squad bay stuffing cookies and candy in their mouths and Morse giving them their instructions. "You will stuff as much of that poogie bait in your mouths as you possibly can. I don't care if you look like a damn squirrel, you will eat all that's in your mouth's and you have only 30 seconds to do it. Ready Go! Faster, Faster! Chew, damn it! I sure as hell don't want to give you mouth to mouth with all that shit in your mouths. Time's up! Are you ladies fucking happy now?" "Sir, No Sir!" "Bullshit! Mommy thought you shitheads just could not live without her cookies and candy, Right!" "Sir, Yes Sir!" These turds were none the worse for wear. They had eaten a hell of a lot of poogie bait in the 30 seconds, but let me tell you, the whole time they were stuffing all that shit in their mouths, they sure seemed as if they were enjoying the hell out of it.

"Ladies we have a winner! You won't believe which one of you maggots won the Hog Board contest, you all voted for Pizza Faces' Hog! Pizza Face! Get your zit ass up here!" "Sir, Pizza Face reporting ordered Sir!" "Your girl's picture has been voted as the best-looking Hog of the whole platoon. I still think you paid some gal to send you her picture. I can't believe an ugly looking turd like you has such a good-looking girl. Mouse, get me another chair and put it next to ours. You, Zit Juice now have the honor of sitting with us in front of the classroom. Sit down! You comfortable?" "Sir extremely," "Extremely my ass, you trying to get smart with me?" "Sir, No Sir!" I understand some of you girls think you can imitate us? Is that Right?" "Sir, Yes Sir," shouted the platoon. "OK, lets see how good you shitheads are."

Like coaches with their teams before the big game, we knew that some of the tension before qualification day had to be taken off the recruits. We also knew that when they thought our backs were turned some of the recruits liked to imitate us, we had done the same thing when we were recruits. Tonight, we would let these makeshift actors perform openly. They had come up with different skits, mainly one of them pretending to be one of us and how we sounded when we dressed down a recruit. It was funny as hell and I had to admit, as always, they had our act down pat. The privates got a big kick out of this and were all rolling with laughter as we allowed them to mock us. The same thing was going on in the rest of the series and I could not think of any better way to relieve their pressure.

"Skits over, OK killers," spoke the Plt. Cmdr." Tomorrow is qualification day, we will see if you earn the right to wear a shooting badge on your uniforms, that is of course if you graduate from boot camp. You all have the skills and the talent to make it happen, you have been firing all week, you know what to do, sight alignment, sight picture, trigger squeeze. We have helped you all we can, and I know that we can depend on you to do it. If you feel shaky that's to be expected. All we want is for you to do your best, nothing less will be accepted or tolerated. As time goes on you will understand that the Marine Corps is a family of trust and confidence, we must trust each other and have the confidence that we know our jobs. I want all of you to leave the squad bay and fall in just below where the choirboys sang. Do It!"

The recruits formed outside, we were on the second deck, where the choirboys had sung after the Gunny's eulogy. What we were about to do was something that crazy fucking Tagleri had started a few platoons back and for some ungodly reason had become a series tradition. Looking down at the recruits, the Plt. Cmdr. tells them "As I said we must all depend on each other that's what the Corps is all about. We must have a trust and confidence that is expected in no other sector of society, the D.I.s and I will now jump from here and we have the confidence and trust that your

sorry asses will catch us. My question to you all is Can You Do It?"
"Sir, Yes Sir!" The Boss then up and jumps off the second story and
we like dumb shits do the same thing. We are even joined by the
Series Gunns, I feel sorry for him because he will go to each platoon in the series and do this shit four times. Naturally we are
caught by our recruits unharmed. Or you would not be reading
this story. I must confess everytime we did this stunt I could not
help wonder if one of our turds might just say. Let's see if these
crazy bastards are really Gods. Or I wonder if they can fly, or gee I
bet they will bounce real high if we let them hit the deck. In any
case, this sure had a way of letting the turds and served as a real
good reminder to me, that when the going really gets rough,
whether in combat or training all we really had was each other.

This tradition of jumping motivated the hell out of the recruits and by the time we were ready for lights out, they were
ready for anything. "Good Night you bunch of killers!" "Good
Night Sir!"

"My herd does its thing in the morning" were the first words
Perez said as he walked into Mimiaga's Hut. "They better do their
thing cause the last time I saw your group of targets in the air, there
was so many Maggies Drawers being waved, it looked like a department store skivvy sale." "Hey Navarre," asks Ssgt Yordt, how's your
mouse doing with your coffee. Yordt never missed a day harassing our
boss about the now infamous coffee cup caper. Remember? earlier in
the training Morse and I, had made the mouse practice grabbing a
coffee cup very quickly off the field desk. Telling him that "The Plt
Cmdr likes things done very fast and efficient" The Boss had come
into the duty hut the following morning and asked the mouse for a
cup of coffee, the Mouse yells "Aye Aye Sir," and like lightning snatches
the cup. The little shit did not realize that there was still coffee in the
cup. The coffee spills all over the Boss and he really gets pissed, he was
so pissed that he starts to stutter and stammer. "What the Hell! Are
you out of your mind, you crazy turd?" Yordt who happen to see the
whole scene, starts laughing his ass off, which of course makes the
Boss even more furious, "Sir, the private was told that the Plt. Cmdr.

likes things done very quickly." "Who the fuck told you that shit?" "Sir, Drill Instructor Sgt. Hernandez and Sgt. Morse." "They did?" "Sir, Yes Sir!" "Get the hell out of my sight Mouse before I stuff your ass in a wall locker" "Aye Aye Sir!" Yordt still laughing told the Boss, how we had the Mouse practice this coffee cup snatching. The Boss had reamed us a new asshole, but after we heard the story from Yordt, about how the Boss had reacted, Shit! it was worth the ass chewing. But now the Boss remembering the incident all over again, gave us that, I still owe you one look. Sure, we loved to harass each other, yet the majority of these duty hut sessions were spent in how to better train our recruits.

At this stage of their training, we rarely had major discipline problems. Those recruits since weeded out or attitudes adjusted by our constant prodding and the ability to send them to the motivation platoon "I'll have your ass making little rocks out of big ones if you keep up with your cheap shit". Even so, it was not uncommon for us to discuss our concerns over individual recruit. "I just don't know how to get through to Private . . .I have tried everything I know and he seems to try hard enough, but just doesn't seem to grasp or retain anything he's taught." This would be an example of our rocks. They seemed to be the type of recruit that weighed most heavily on our minds. These were the recruits that seemed to try very hard but for whatever reasons did not seem to be smart enough to retain much of the instruction they were given. This should never have happen, because all recruits were tested prior to us getting them. They were suppose to meet basic criteria of intelligence prior to entering the Corps, sometimes the testing was not a true evaluation of their abilities or lack of ability. We had our own methods of helping these rocks, we provided added instruction, other recruits helped them, and we even had an academic platoon or section on the Depot. With all this added help they eventually were able to get to the point where they could regurgitate all the required responses. But you could tell that they had no idea what the hell they were talking about. We could recycle them to another series to see if they could get their shit together, which would add a few weeks to their training time. After we had tried everything we would inform the Series Officer about the recruit's shortfalls, always supported with documentation on what we had done to remedy the situation. The final decision would be left to the Lieutenant as to whether or not he would recommend further processing for discharge. Our problem was that since these young men tried so very hard and were able to parrot the correct response maybe we should just say the hell with it and graduate them anyway. Like I said, they could give the right answer but ask him why for example the first step in our first aid instruction was to check the breathing and he would look at you with a blank stare. He knew it was the first step and would say, " Sir the first live saving step is to check the breathing" "Why?" at this point we would probably get just continue to stare at you with that blank look. "To see if the shithead is still alive, you dipshit." Sure we could graduate them. But we knew that our Corps was not just a bunch of robots, able only to parrot information, we were a thinking group of trained professionals, able to make and more importantly allowed to made decisions because of our experience, training and education provided by our Corps.

This was a side of us the recruits never saw, we did not have the luxury of showing any indecisiveness in front of them. The final decision might rest with the L.T., but the ball started rolling with the recommendation from one of us Hats. This was a responsibility not taken lightly, and we had to ensure that we weighed all factors, tried everything and most important, not allow sympathy for the recruit to cloud or decision.

Although we had these discussions quite frequently, pre-qual night was not a night for this type of discussion. Since all of us had to be present for qualification day, Mimiaga's hut was jammed full with all of us, this was a night to bullshit each other on how much better our platoons would do than the others. Yep, the coffee was hot and the air was thick with our cigarette smoke. Seemed to be even thicker with all the shit that was being thrown around. "Let me tell you one thing, my platoon is so good they might not even make it to graduation, they will probably be snatched up by the Marine Corps Rifle Team, before Boot Camp is even over" Yep, and then they will be called Sammy's Snipers." "You better hope that they're snatched up, cause the way you train turds and as shitty as your herd looks the L.T. will probably fire your dumb ass and send you through Boot Camp all over again," says Tag, "Right Gunny?" "You're all full of shit, back when I was a recruit," "Yeah, we know the rest of the story Gunny, In the Old Corps Right!" "Damn straight, in the Old Corps, we didn't have none of this easy stuff you and these turds have to do." A D.I. in those days was one mean S.O.B." "Sure gunny and you had to qualify with a slingshot. I'll tell you all one damn thing right now, and that is you can all kiss my beautiful Hawaiian Portuguese Ass! Further more, now that I have got all of you perverts excited at that thought, lets cut the chatter and call it a night. Me and Mimiaga have a serious game of chess and I don't want the rest of you to screw us up, with all your talk about how great your goats are. So get the hell out of here, tomorrow will be a long day." "Aye Aye Gunny, we're otta here!" "Hey, you know what Gunns?" "What is it now?" "Since you mentioned it, you do have kind of a nice ass," says Tag as he runs out the hatch, before the Gunny can snatch him up.

"Range Cadence Count!" At this command the platoon would now sound off with each marching step, "Breathe, Relax, Aim., Slack, Squeeze, Pow, Bulls eye, Sir!" "Louder I can't hear you! Once again killers, Range Cadence Count!" Yeah that right let me hear it! Platoon Halt! Today is the day sweeties, you will earn the right to wear a shooting badge, Right!" "Sir, Yes Sir!" The Plt Cmdr has a few things to tell you, so listen up. "Just remember everything you were taught. No butt pulling for you today, another platoon from another series will be pulling your targets. That's to make sure everything stays on the up and up. Its all up to you now, Can you do it?" "Sir, Yes Sir!" "I said can you do it?" "Sir, Yes Sir!" "It's show time so move it out and lets rock and roll."

Like the Boss said it was now up to the recruits, we could only watch them as they fired, but that did not mean we would not be everywhere, going from one recruit to another before they went up to the firing line. Keeping scores after each string of fire, seeing how well each recruit was doing, watching to see how many points might be needed in each string of fire to qualify. The L.T. and the Gunny were watching from the center of the line in full dress uniform. This was to motivate the recruits. Naturally they both were Rifle Experts and wearing the Expert Badges, so the recruits could see them. The same badges they too could wear, once earned. Oh Well, it was all up to the individual private, all we could do was add a little encouragement. The type of encouragement depended on the situation. "What the Hell is your problem? Looks like somebody stepped on your crank!" "Sir, the private is nervous Sir!" "Nervous! What the hell for? You have had the best rifle training in the entire world. Now son, just shoot the way you have been taught and I bet I won't see anything but Bull Eyes, Right!" "Sir, Yes Sir!" "OK, show me how it's done. Up and down the line we went, "Sir the Private is worried Sir," "Worried! Bet you need a little motivation and tightening up, don't you?" "Sir, Yes Sir!" This may sound crazy, but the recruits that asked for a little tightening up to help them battle their nervous tension, were actually asking for a choke. "OK, come here, Ready?" "Sir. Yes Sir!" "Feel Better!" "Sir, Yes Sir!," No shit, probably over half the platoon asked for a quick taste of motivation. But what was really funny was that it worked!

"Cease fire on the firing line! Shooters that was our last string of Slow Fire. Is the firing line secure? Are the Butts secure? The firing line and the butts are now secured. Drill Instructors form up your platoons, the Range is now Secured." "Fall In!" We now had to rush our herds, because the remainder of this day would be very hectic. The recruits would now have to clean their weapons, go to chow and pack up all their gear for our return trip back to San Diego on the next day. They and we would have little time to reflect back on the rifle scores. We had done very well, only two of the privates had failed to qualify with their weapons. You would have thought this would be a good time for more harassment from us, but nothing we could do would make the two non-quals feel any worse than they already did. They knew that Marines were noted for their ability to fire the rifle. And since all Marines needed to qualify each year with their weapon, if they graduated from Boot Camp, they would have another chance to earn a shooting badge. This provided little consolation, in the meantime the world would know they were non-shooters because of the lack of a shooting badge on their uniform.

"Ladies you now have your scores and the Plt Cmdr has informed me that Plt Cmdr Ssgt Yordts' platoon had the overall best score of the series. That means girls, that they took the range! For you maggots that did not do as well as they had hoped, its over now, nothing can be done about it, so I best not see any of you feeling sorry for yourself. A Marine learns from his mistakes and continues to March Forward with a full 30-inch step. No fucking Half steps in this life. Right!" "Sir, Yes Sir!" "We have a lot of shit to get done, not only will we be going back to San Diego, the Series Officer has decided we will go for a little walk before we get on the buses. It's only a little 20-mile walk and we step off at 0630. I don't see any problem, Do you see any problems, Sweeties?" "Sir, No Sir!"

With all of our shit packed and ready to be transported back to MCRD San Diego. The recruits showered and in their racks, this long day finally over meant another milestone in our training was over and behind us. Now we had to listen to Ssgt Yordt and Tagleri's bullshit of being number one platoon on the Range. "Hernandez, as always, I think you owe me a few cold ones at the Anchor says Tag as he walks and sits his ass down in my Duty Hut. "Big deal! Your herd beat us by a cunt's hair and now I have to listen to your cheap shit until I beat your ass with the next herd." "Damn Straight, everyday and all the way, but wait till I find Perez, he will never hear the end of it. Especially with his crap about Sammy's Snipers." "You go ahead and talk shit, we still have the rest of final events back at Diego." "And my herd will blow your ass away on the rest of the events." "In your dreams, compardre!" "Maybe, but I sure hope they are wet ones!" "What's the scuttlebutt on our little march? "The L.T. says we step off at 0630 and then route step to San Onofre, Good idea, because I also heard that starting with our next herd, we will start taking the recruits through their basic infantry training, adding two more weeks to Boot Camp." "Yeah and you are just going to eat the shit right up." "Ah Ooh Rah! You know it! Makes fucking sense, to do it this way, after all the turds are here on Pendleton any damn way." "See Ya in the morning for our little walk, Semper Fi." "You got it, Do or Die!"

We had now covered the first five miles of our twenty with the L.T. in the lead followed by the four platoons in our series. We were marching in order of how well each platoon had done on the Range. Yordt's herd, ours Mimiaga's and Ssgt Bosch's. The end platoon would be eating the dust created by the recruits up front. The roads were very dusty and believe me 400 privates can make a lot of dust. But, I have to tell you, it was a sight to behold. We were in a column of two's recruits on each side of the road and the D.I.'s in the middle. As always we were going up and down the line of our turds, the rifle range fast becoming nothing but a memory. It was still early morning with the Pacific Ocean on our left and the towering hills of Camp Pendleton on our right, we were calling cadence and the recruits were singing Marching Songs.

"Let me hear it! You bunch of dirt covered Devil Dogs!" "I put my hand upon her thigh, Yo, Ho, Yo, Ho, I put my hand upon her thigh, and she said Marine your mighty sly, Yo, Ho, . . .I know a girl all dressed in green and she ain't nothing but a sex machine . . .I was born in San Diego, in the land that God forgot, the sand is eighteen inches deep and the sun is blazing hot, I run a hundred miles or more and never ask to stop . . .G.I. beans and G.I. gravy, Gee I wished I joined the Navy, Bullshit Marine Corps . . .I don't know but I've been told Eskimo pussy is mighty cold" . . .We had a million songs, and to hear 400 voices singing while we marched through the hills, all I can say it was just fucking beautiful!

We would break for chow at the fifteen-mile mark, but in the interim, it was eat the dirt, sing the songs, and us mocking the recruits. "Lard Ass!" "Sir Lard Ass, reporting as ordered Sir!" "How much weight have you lost?" "Fifteen pounds Sir!"

"Lean and Mean, Mommy isn't going to recognize you, we might have to enter your ass in a Mr. Universe Contest!" "Where is Dumbo Ears?" "Sir, Dumbo Ears," "You like this little walk don't you?" "Sir, yes Sir!" Shit, I should have your tired ass run up one of those hills and see if you can catch the wind and glide for the next few miles." "House Mouse!" "Sir!" " Run up to the front of the Series just to let our Series Officer know, how glorious this day is in the U. S. Marine Corps!" "Aye Aye Sir!" The L.T. would have numerous recruits sent up to him by each of the D.I.'s to let him know how great it was to be alive and in the United States Marine Corps. The L.T. would just comment and tell the recruit to" Carrying on Private" with that smile on his face as he led his series on our little march. "Secretary!" "Sir!" We are surrounded by various plants, you being a college boy, I wonder if you can tell me the Latin Name for good old common RagWeed?" "Sir, the private does not know Sir!" "What! You don't know, what kind of college did you go to? College my ass you were just trying to get out of the damn draft!" "Sir, No Sir!" "Well, then you didn't learn a damn thing, everyone knows that the Latin Name for RagWeed is Ragous Weedous, you dipshit, Now go up to the Series Officer and let him know what you have just learned!" "Aye Aye Sir!"

Reaching the fifteen-mile mark, we broke for chow, and the recruits had another treat in store for them C-rations! Meals in a can, issued in little boxes. We had distributed them throughout the series before the march, now we would have to show the turds how to eat them. First you open your can of crackers with your C-ration opener we call a John Wayne. You now have a empty can, this can will be used for your stove, you will place you heat tab in this can, that way you can heat up all the other shit that came in the boxes. Now you will open your can of meat, beans and franks, ham and lima's or whatever you got. Understood? You will cut the top only three quarters of the way and then bend it out. You now have a handle, cause we would not want any of you to burn your little hands. Contained in the box is also a brown packet, it has all kinds of goodies in it. Shit paper, spoon, gum, (Which you will not chew), cigarettes, matches, etc. But I have the most important item anyone can have to eat their rations properly. It's this bottle of Tabasco Sauce. This sauce is what will make your rations "Out Fucking Standing to Eat". I have out of the goodness of my military heart, purchased 10 bottles of sauce just for you ladies. Understood!" "Sir, Yes Sir!" "Get to it and break for chow! I will be dining with Drill Instructors Sgt.'s Tagleri and Perez." Joining Tag, and Sammy, the first item of business was to make our C-ration coffee, that done and sitting back with that can of coffee in hand we not only could see our herds but the entire series setting in for chow. They were dust covered, dirty, tired and wolfing down their chow like they would never get another meal. It looked like some damn Hollywood Movie, and I kept thinking that it would be less than three months and these recruits would probably be eating their rations, in the same way. Dirty, tired, hungry but with one big difference, their eyes would constantly scan the countryside, weapons would never be more than a arms length away and this meal would seem like a picnic in the park. They would have many such meals in the Nam. I could tell that the same thoughts were crossing the minds of Tag and Sammy. None of this was new to any of us, and being in the field, eating rations could bring back alot of memories for all of us. "Sir, Guide requests permission to speak to the Drill Instructor?" "What Guide?" "Sir, many of the privates are in need of a head call, Sir!" "Hey, Sgt. Tagleri! Did you hear that shit, the turds need to go potty, I bet they are wondering were the port a potties are at!"

"Is that right, Guide?" "Sir, Yes Sir!" "Listen up! No port a potties around here, we will have to teach you field expedite measures or how to shit in the field. You will take your E-tool, (Entrenching shovel) and then you will make a small hole, we call it a Cat Hole. You will then squat and do your thing and just like a cat cover it up. Don't forget to wipe your ass, and watch out for snakes. Sooo those of you that need to make a head call, spread out and fertilize my beloved Camp Pendleton, those that just need to piss, look for the nearest bush that appears to need water and the make it rain! While the recruits started to spread out, I could hear the raspy voice of Ssgt Mimiaga as he screamed at one of his recruits. From his screaming all I could gather was that he had been eating chow with the L.T. and the Series Gunns, those two were now laughing to the point of tears. I had to find out what the hell was going on! As I approached the three of them I then spotted the subject of Mimaga's screams, a recruit about twenty yards away from them. He had his E-tool in one hand, his trousers and skivvies were down around his knees, and he was trying very hard to stand at the position of attention. Mimaga just keeps yelling at him, "I told you that I was a personal friend of the almighty. You didn't believe me, Did You, You fucking maggot! I bet you know better Now, don't you!" "Sir, Yes Sir!" Mimaga screaming even louder to his platoon "All of you turds, now know the awesome power of your Plt. Cmdr. Don't You?" "I can't hear You!" "Sir, Yes Sir!" I finally reached the L.T. and the Series Gunns, "What the hell happen!" "The L.T. could only keep shaking his head and laugh while the Gunns told the story. You won't believe it! "See that Oak tree lying over there, as he pointed to a small oak about ten feet long on the ground. This turd comes up while we were eating chow and requests permission to make a head call, seems he just can't wait. Mimiaga tells this goat he had one hell of a nerve to interrupt his noon meal. Especially since he was dining with the Series Officer and me, and that he really had a set of balls to ask for any damn thing since he was a non-qual. You puke face he says, you ask about taking a shit, while I'm eating and enjoying my meal, how crude can you be. Since you have already interrupted I will grant your request, you will go over to that oak tree and with good cover and concealment, dig your cat hole. I do not want to see your bare ass, Understood! You will then squat in a military manner, back straight, no slouching and then you will commence to do your thing. You will grunt only three times! Private if you screw up any of the procedures I have outlined for you, I will then ask my personal friend, the man upstairs, to fell that tree on your scummy body. Do you Understand?" "Sir, Yes Sir!"

"This maggot then does an about face and goes over to the tree like he was told. The next thing, we hear this god-awful cracking sound and the tree starts to fall, this turd jumps out from under the tree, eyes bigger than shit and looks straight at Mimaga, shouting "Sir the Private did not do anything Wrong!" Mimiaga shouts back 'Bullshit! I knew you would screw things up and I told you what would happen," You heard the rest. We had to put up with Mimagas bullshit for the rest of the march about how he and the almighty, were as tight as fleas on a dog, and he could have trees just fall over because of his connections with the Man Upstairs. We of course asked him to perform these feats again, but his answer was he had to save his power. But No Shit, this really did happen!

Our march was finally over and we reached San Onofre without any other incidents, and the privates and we were ready to go back to San Diego. Pendleton was now behind us and now it was back to MCRD and the damn airplanes.

PHASE I
GRADUATION

The recruits had only six weeks left until graduation day. The next six weeks of training would be in preparation for the last phase of training and then their graduation. We would have to prepare for all the final events, consisting of Academic tests, physical fitness test, uniform inspection, practical application and final drill competition. As usual we had no time to waste, once the privates stepped off the bus at MCRD, all our energy and theirs would be dedicated to achieving the best possible results in the final events. The upcoming days would be hectic and intense, with no time to spare, but these were not the same young men we had met on the yellow footprints. They were now considered to be a Senior Series. More importantly, a metamorphosis had taken place among them. No longer were they that Rag Tag bunch of maggots we had first met and started to train. They were all stronger, more confident, those that needed to lose weight, had lost it, those that needed to gain weight had gained it, they knew what was expected of them and consequently would also now expect more from us. It was no longer hippty hop Mob Stop. Now they responded as one person, the new recruits on the Depot now looked at them with awe. Their D.I.s now pointed at our platoons telling their recruits the same thing we had told these young men early on in their training. "Maybe, just Maybe you turds will be able to march like that Platoon". No they were not Marines by any stretch of the imagination, nor would they be addressed as such but they and we could see the light at the end of the tunnel.

Yeah, MCRD with all those damn planes was a pain in the ass, but I have to admit it was good to be back. I had not been to the Anchor in over two weeks and it I sure as hell would not have a whole lot of time now, with final events just around the corner but at least I might be able to get a few Happy Hours under my belt. Since preparation for final events would tax our time almost as much as the first few weeks after picking up the herd, Tag, myself , Morse and Perez had made up for our loss of Anchor time last night. It was a tradition in our series that all the Plt Cmdrs took the first night of duty when we returned from the Range. Damn good idea, it left all of us Junior Hats with the time to party hearty. It also followed the age-old Marine Corps maxim of looking out for your men and their welfare.

We had a great time, telling lies over a few cold ones, we even decided to get some chow between our brews. You know just grab a couple of burgers, then go back to the Anchor, see if any women had decided to venture out. The burger place was just down the street, the one with the Clown in front and you can just drive right through and place your order. Now I don't know of any self-respecting D.I., with a couple of brews under his belt that could possibly resist the urge to harass the Clown. "May I take your order this damn Clown says . . ." "Orders I give the damn orders, Let me tell you one thing!" " What?" "I can't hear you! Speak Up! and where in the hell did you get that Nose. Looks like a red neon sign! You look like a few days on the fat farm would do you a world of good. I told you I give the orders! Think it's funny, you best wipe that smile of your face!" Much to the relief of the Clown and the servers, we finally placed our orders and got our chow and went on our merry way. It wasn't the first time we had tried to get the Clown squared away and I'm sure as close as this place was to the Anchor that we were not the first Hats to screw with the Clown. I have to admit the Clown was a big challenge, because he never did wipe that damn smile off his face!

We had a great time, but now it was time to get back to work. The recruits were now billeted in the new barracks, another privilege given to the senior series. These barracks were just like the barracks at Edson Range. Except when they were built, some dipshit decided it would be great to have white tile placed on the decks (floor) instead of our favorite Marine Corps Green. Sure it looked pretty, but the problem was that the recruits and their boots would scuff the hell out of this white tile. These black scuffmarks were not acceptable, so we had to become very innovative to avoid these marks. We first had the privates remove their boots, even these few minutes ate into our training time, so we finally came up with the brilliant idea of having them wear slip on covers, much like the Doctors wear over their shoes. It proved to be the best method and no more damn scuff marks. All of this could have been avoided if the Dip that contracted for the tile would have only realized what 80 to 100 men going in and out of the barracks would do to white tile. Jeez, Oh Well, Semper Fi!

The change in recruits from the early days of training was so dramatic and even if it did take place with every platoon, it still never failed to amaze me. The privates now seemed eager to learn all that they could possibly learn from us. Reaching the point even among themselves of not tolerating anything less than perfection. Overheard conversations and even their speech seemed to mimic ours. "Bullshit that's not good enough! Come on you can do it! Reach down and see if you have a set of balls between those legs! Almost does not hack it! Do or Die Semper Fi!" No longer were their individual concerns about themselves the most important things in their lives, it was now the Platoon, the stronger helping the weaker, the smarter helping the not so smart. They were now pulling together forming a cohesive unit of men, and with this eagerness to learn it also seemed as if now they were actually pushing us. Pit calls would become few and far between at this stage of training, they would still screw up, and the choke became our prime method of correction.

Our nightly classroom sessions became more and more a question and answer period of what would take place after Boot Camp and about the Marine Corps in general. "If you graduate you will be a basically qualified Marine. You will then continue your training for whatever MOS you have been assigned to learn your job in the Corps.

Many of you will then probably go to the NAM. Because of the training that you have received you will be prepared for whatever the Corps has in store for you. As long as you keep your heads out of your asses and practice all that you have learned and will learn, you should have no problem. Always remember one thing, at this point in time you are Privates, lowest of the nine enlisted ranks in the Corps, lower than whale shit, but if you graduate you will have accomplished one thing that no one, no where can take away from you. You are a United States Marine, you then become part of legacy as the finest fighting force in the entire world. No one Marine did anything alone, we are a band of brothers, looking out for one another all the time. You will never be alone as long as there is a fellow Marine by your side. When we have to go to battle it is because we have been ordered to go! We at that point do our job, regardless of political opinion. We do what we have been trained to do! When you look left or right it will be your fellow Marine's that you see and you will be confident in the knowledge that he or she will be looking out for you and you for them. That's just the way it is and the way it should be! Understand! Those little bullshit civilian jobs you might have had in the past. And even large corporations don't train you to take the jobs of the Boss, we train you to take our jobs, we pass on all our knowledge, we don't jealousy guard our knowledge for fear that you might become better or take our jobs. **You are trained to lead, and it's not look out for yourself, its look out for the men and women in your care.** That's the reason, ladies we don't let anyone else screw with you. That's also the reason if you have not noticed, when we go to chow, you shit heads always eat first, when you get rank you also get privileges, the most important privilege is that you have the ability to look out for the men and women in your care. The book calls it "Looking out for your men and their welfare", we call it just plain loyalty! Loyalty to yourself, your Marines, your country, your God, and your Corps. Loyalty is also a two way street. Do you girls understand!" "Sir Yes Sir!" "Don't ask your men to do anything you won't do yourself. Small things will mean a lot when you finally get out into the Corps and you obtain some rank. Just think about what you can do. If you have your troops in formation, you face the Sun not them, they eat first so if you run out of chow, its you that goes without! **You lead by your example!** As worthless as you seem to be right now, I fucking doubt if any of you have to worry about any of this shit! But mark my words, if any of you shitheads amount to anything in the Corps and you fuck up I will certainly hear about it, and I will personally get on a fucking plane, walk or crawl just to choke your scummy ass! Is that also Understood!" "Sir Yes Sir!" "I can't hear You!"

As with every platoon the days before final events just seemed to run into one another. It seemed as if we had just returned from the range and now we only had two weeks left before these events. The recruits had already been to the base tailor and had been fitted for all their uniforms. Up until now the only uniform they had was their utility uniform and boots. Now they had finally received their full issue of our uniforms and accessories. The fitting process was something I always enjoyed. You could see that gleam come into the turds eyes, they would suck in their gut and push out their chest as the tailor made his marks for cutting and sewing. It reminded me of what some gal might go through on her first real date. You could almost read the thought process of the recruits. "Wait till they see me back home in my uniform" They were constantly reminded that the only reason the Marine's Uniform meant a damn thing to the general public, was because of the legacy of those Marine's who had worn the uniform before them. This was a legacy that they would inherit, and they had best live up to the standards set by those former Marines. Our proud history had been won in many battles with blood, sweat and yes tears.

This was a cycle that would not allowed to be broken. Because some shithead graduated from recruit training when we should have shit canned his ass from the Corps. We, the Hats, overseen by our commanders, were tasked with the job to make sure this did not happen!

"Lights Out!" "Sir, Lights Out, Aye Aye Sir!" "Tonight I want to hear my prayer favorite prayer, Ladies!" "Sir, I am the Eagle globe and Anchor, a symbol inanimate, words to are symbols inanimate but capable of conveying thoughts and ideas. I am through this symbol, the physical embodiment of patriotism, courage and devotion to duty, I am in body fact and spirit soon to be a United States Marine." "Well done girls!" "Good Night!" "Good Night Sir!" The recruits again bedded down for the night and I had to admit I was pretty much played out. The Series had finished their Physical Fitness Test, requiring the privates to do a series of pull-ups, sit-ups and then a three mile endurance run, with us leading the platoon. This was probably the easiest of all the final events, because at this stage of training we had taken the recruits on many a run and naturally they had been subjected to numerous push-ups as a motivational tool when they screwed up. They had run the obstacle course, bayonet training all this and their constant marching, while carrying their weapons had put them in the best physical shape of their lives.

Played out or not I had to have my coffee with the other Hats on duty, Ssgt Yordt's hut was our meeting place for tonight's bull session. Tag and Perez were already in his hut when I arrived. "What Up?" "Looks like the Series did pretty well on the PT test, we have some real studs in the group, just about all the turds did their maximum of 20 pull-ups and maxed out the timed sit-ups." "What a helluva difference from when we picked this batch up from the yellow footprints." "Shit, I can remember that half of them were puking their guts out on the first run, some were not even capable of lifting their own bodies up for one pull-up." "They fell on their asses on the obstacle course, afraid to climb the ropes and watching them try and scale the different obstacles is always funny at the start of training. It is amazing how much of a difference just twelve weeks makes, when you get these people away from civilian life and mommy's apron strings. Like I always say, the more you pit them the stronger they get," says Sammy." "Not much longer with this herd anyway, chimed in Tag, "and we get to start all over again." Talking about the next herd, I heard scuttlebutt that instead of us taking them on their 3 mile run with rifles, boots and utes. They will run their own three miles in tennis shoes and shorts." "No Way! I can't believe the Corps will change the way they do the PT test. Tennis shoes and jock straps, bullshit!" "I'm just telling you what I heard! "The L.T. was telling the Series Gunns, not only will the recruits take the test in this gear, but the whole Marine Corps will take the PT test the same way." "Now that I think about it, its OK by me, need to work I my tan any damn way. You know how the women love to see my tanned body!" "Sammy you are so full of shit, you come up with more crap than anyone I know, Scuttlebutt should be your middle name." Tennis shoes, Ha! next you will be telling us that yelling at the turds and calling them names will be outlawed. As interesting as all of this is, it don't mean nothing, we have final drill, junk on the bunk, practical and final inspection all in the next 4 days." "All of you know," says Sammy again," that my herd will probably take all the final events." "Yeah, like your herd took the range! What happen to Sammys Sniper's? Boy now that was a crock of shit." "Well all of you can crock this," says Sammy as he gives us the finger.

As always we will just take it all day by day, its just about all over for this series but the fat lady singing, come graduation day, it will be just like any other herd. "Their Mommy's won't even recognize half of them." "You're right, it sure doesn't take them long to snap out of their civilian bullshit." "They don't even seem to realize the change. They all come from basically the same mold. Never had to really challenge themselves, when they were tired they could just quit and no one made a big deal out of it. Now they have to push themselves like never in their lives or answer to us crazy Hats or visit the pits. We don't listen to any of their crybaby crap, Sir I can't, I'm tired, it hurts, I don't like eggs to eat or whatever, one things for sure with all the excuses they have this job is never dull. They sure can come up with a lot of bullshit and we only have thirteen weeks to make them Marines. Some of them carry a lot of old baggage. You know what I mean. The country boy, who has never seen the big city, city kids that think they are so street wise, white turds never having shared a meal with blacks, or vice versa, some as dumb as rocks, college boys that think they know everything. Most had no idea what the hell they were getting into. I bet the over half of them have never been in a fight, yet in a few months they will be in a War. We have to get them to pull together, in their civilian life they were all going in different directions, probably no goals in life, didn't care about a damn thing except their own individual wants and needs. Now look at them, they all have the same goal, it's the platoon over their individual crap. Like with every herd, they sure are a far cry from that bunch of clowns we gave Hippty hop mob stop too"

We command Platoon Halt, and they stop on a dime, we say jump and we hear, "How high Sir!" The other day I saw three of my turds marching from chow and I Yelled, "You three, half of you come here!" "Shit if they did not actually try to split themselves in half to obey the order." "But if you shitheads remember, they are no different than they way we were." "Bullshit I was never as fucked up as some of these maggots." "My dying ass, when I was a turd I screwed up so much shit, I thought I was going to have permanent finger marks around my neck." "Me too" says Tag. I'm surprised the Corps did not put a memorial of some type in the Pit area, I was in the Pits so damn much. But just like these screwballs, we finally started to get our shit in one bag." Right now we could tell any one of our herds that we had orders to march them through the gates of Hell and all we would hear is "Aye Aye Sir!" "Fucking A," says Tag, "Fucking A!"

All of this talk was very interesting but it was time for me to hit the rack. As odd as it might seem to you, that our discussion turned so philosophical this was they way it was at the end of the training cycle of every herd. I don't know if it was our way of beginning to accept these young men that we had trained, into the brotherhood of the Corps or if it was our way of starting to let them go. The latter we would never admit too, we would call melancholy bullshit, but I truly believe that was the main reason for these types of discussions. Know matter how you looked at it, for the last thirteen weeks we had become their whole world. We had become their Mother's, Father's,

Sister's and Brother's and the graduation of any of these maggots was like saying good-bye to a family member. We, from our own recruit days, knew that Boot Camp and the D.I.'s, was an experience that would never be forgotten.

"Boss!, everything's ready for the JOB (Junk on the Bunk), the privates are putting on their set of starched utilities and getting ready for you to take them to final drill." A JOB, was the inspection of all the clothing and accessories the recruits had been issued from socks to uniforms, all of these items placed on their racks (bunks). The privates had been preparing for this inspection all morning and half the damn night. The purpose of this inspection was to ensure that the recruits had their full issue of clothing and all their gear. Our preparation for this inspection was an assembly line of irons, and folding stations. You see, everything had to be placed on the rack and folded to a specific size, skivvy shirts had to be folded to six inches and placed on the rack one on the other so you could read the turds name marked on the inside of the collar. This folding and placement applied to all articles the recruits owned, and when placed on the rack it would be in accordance with the Marine Corps Guidebook for a JOB. Yep, the Corps even had regulations on how, what and where even your skivvies were to be placed for an inspection. Not only did the placement of these articles have to be perfect for each individual but also all the racks had to be identical and each item lined up perfectly with the other articles on the other racks. We had to take the step by step approach.

"Ladies! now take your skivvy shirts, they will be placed 18 inches from the head of the rack on the inboard side and four inches from the side of the rack. Do It!" This procedure was done for each and every article, we would name it, tell them what we wanted and then have them do it, then as always check it, and check it again. After the placement of each article, we would have them take a long string. And place it so that you could look down the line of racks and see that each particular article not only was on the rack in the right location but it also was aligned perfectly with each item on any rack to the right or left. JOB was considered to be a final event, so we did everything we could to outshine the other platoons in the series. We marked our gear in black paint instead of ink because it was darker and stood out better, even the soles of the boots or shoes not in use were polished. Tricks of the trade, gained from experience and passed on to the recruits. We didn't let them touch any of their brass already shined with their fingers. OK ladies, now that you have shined your extra belt buckle, take your handkerchief and taking great care not to touch the brass with your scummy hands place it on the rack. Take your rulers and measure two inches from you cover now take your buckle and place it at the two inch mark and centered left to right on your covers." I know all this sounds like a pain in the ass, but any Marine Corps Inspection is never to be taken lightly. We knew that the emphasis we placed on the inspections the recruit had while in training would also be the emphasis the recruits would place on any subsequent inspections they might have while in the Corps. The privates had become as familiar with Q-tips, brasso, toothbrushes and all the other cleaning items as they had with their own weapons.

While the Plt Cmdrs took their herds to the final drill competition, the rest of us had to remain back to greet the Inspection Teams for the Junk on the Bunk. Once they arrived we took notes, because no matter how well prepared, they always seemed to find something wrong. They might be minor items like a piece of clothing off by a quarter of an inch or the infamous Irish Pennants found on the inside of a trouser leg. As we went from one rack to another I knew the boss would be motivating the hell out of our herd for their drill competition. Once again another rung in the ladder to becoming a Marine was to be performed today. This was the unbuttoning of the top button of their Utility Jackets (Shirts). Allowing the recruits to unbutton the top button was just like the ritual of blousing their trousers prior to their first drill competition. They would be halted and told to reach up and unbutton the top button of their utility jacket. I could remember when I was a recruit and what it had meant to be allowed to undo that button. "OK Maggots!" my D.I. had said, "Reach up and unbutton the top button" WOW, it felt like someone had just taken a noose from around my neck, I now was one step closer to becoming a Marine. The only people allowed to have their top button undone, were real Marines or those recruits that had already finished their final drill competition and that meant their graduation was just a few days away. The inspection team was finally finished and had found the usual discrepancies. You know the type! Some ones skivvies were off by a quarter of an inch, a few Irish Pennants, sounds like petty bullshit, but as we had always taught the turds, you must pay attention to detail. If you take care of the little things than the big ones take care of themselves. I remember one Gunny asking me if I had counted the rations for my men. I thought I would be a smart-ass, Gunny they come in cases of 12 rations to a case and I have two cases, makes it 24 in my book and just enough chow for all of us. Bigger than shit some dip back at the factory, only packed 11 in one case. The Gunny just shook his head and said "Guess who goes without chow" Attention to Detail, those rations could just have easily been ammo and than we would have been in a world of hurt. I told this story over and over to the recruits, Attention to Detail!

I walked to the Parade Deck, seems we had drawn the last drill card so the Boss was just taking our herd out for their drill evaluation. Damn, they looked good, top button undone, white skivvy shirt against the green of the jackets, jaws clenched, starched covers, sun light glistening off their spit shined boots, rifles were carried at the port and they were marching as if they were one person, leaning back and strutting.

The Boss put them through their paces, going in and out of each drill movement from the card. Like a fine tuned machine they responded, a green machine, all we needed to make the picture complete was the command of "Fix Bayonets and Charge", God help anything or anyone that might have stood in their path.

It was finally over and when all the drill scores were tallied, Ssgt Yordts herd had taken the drill competition. We came in second, but second don't mean shit. All we had left to be done for the rest of the day was for the privates to take their written and then their practical exams. The written test consisted of everything they had learned in the last thirteen weeks, History of the Corps, First Aid, Drill Movements and Commands, Uniforms, Weapons, Code of Conduct, General Orders etc . . . They would take the written exam but the Corps felt that just cause you were able to pass a written exam did not mean you knew the subject. You then had to demonstrate your ability to apply the subject. The practical exam consisted of 12 different stations. A recruit would report to each station. And would be asked to perform a series of tasks, each selected at random. Each station was manned by a D.I from another series, the recruits might be asked to assemble or disassemble a weapon, perform a series of bayonet movements, execute a proper Salute, perform various first aid measures, anything and everything the recruit needed to know to become a Basic Marine. We naturally had been preparing for all the final events, since our arrival from the Rifle Range. We had set up mock practical stations in the squad bay, given them written exams, we left nothing to chance. I will tell you that as the recruits practiced all of this, a lot of quick motivation was given, You got it! A quick choke worked wonders for student retention. "No, No, you shit for brains, that battle dressing is on wrong, You, Maggot Lips, how the hell you going to place a tourniquet around some ones neck.? Jeez, you will choke him to death. What do you mean you don't remember your fifth general order? Come here, closer asshole so I don't have to reach so far to choke your dumb ass! Feels Good!" "Sir, Yes Sir," "Bet you remember your orders now don't you?" "Sir, Yes Sir!"

The recruits had to obtain at least 80% on the exams in order to pass both the written and practical tests. Although we would not know the official scores until later that day, as with any exam the individual had some idea whether he passed or not and we could tell by the carriage of the recruits that we had no failures.

Failure meant the private would be recycled into another platoon and given one more chance to do it all over again. For the recruit that meant at least another week on the Depot, and as close as they were to graduation that one week could seem like a lifetime. After the exam we had just enough time to get the herd back to the barracks, make a head call and than to evening chow. The Boss had said the L.T. wanted all of us in a series formation after evening chow in front of the Mess Hall. He would give the series the results of the testing. With all the series present we awaited the Series Officer, Series Attention was finally called as the L.T. centered himself if front of us. We could tell from the look on the L.T.'s face that we had done all right. The L.T. addressed the Series, "I can't believe all of you recruits passed both the practical and written exams. Not only did you pass but you averaged a score of 95%." "Ah Roo Ah" Came the thunderous yell from the series. Well I'll be damned, the practice as always had paid off, and of course you never knew until the results were in. "I believe that the series has earned the right to a phone call home." This brought another yell from the turds. The L.T. was trying to motivate the herd, we usually allowed them to make a call on this day anyway but why tell them that, when we could use this as a reward for a job well done. This would be the first time they had been allowed to call home. Naturally they were all hyped up for this and we would march their young asses to the phone center and limited their time to 3 minutes. We still had final inspection and that was on the schedule for 0800 tomorrow morning. After the phone call, the recruits would pack all of the gear that had been laid out for the JOB in seabags, except for one set of utilities and the uniforms they would wear for the final inspection and on graduation.

This was summer and the Marine Corps had different uniforms for each of the seasons so our Inspection would be done in the Tropical Uniform. Again we had prepared for this event and picked up these uniforms from the cleaners a couple of days before. At every opportunity the privates had gone over these uniforms, checking and rechecking for Irish Pennants.

The pressing job of the cleaners was never good enough and our irons were busy to make sure not a wrinkle remained. As with any inspection we were ready, weapons were cleaned, shoes had been spit shined, brass gleaming like a diamond in a goats ass.

A few added tricks of the trade made everything just right. To the shoes already showing a mirror finish we added a little floor wax, this made the shine really stand out, I mean these shoes were so shined that we could tell the color of a gals skivvies if she stood over them. Weapons had been steamed cleaned in the Mess Hall at the cost of $20 slipped to the Mess Sergeant. We had done this a couple of days before drill competition, recruits sneaking in the Mess Hall putting the weapons in the steamer which cleaned the hell out of them. A light coat of Oil and the small area's attacked with Q-tips made them squeaky-clean.

We all had different tricks of the trade, Ssgt Yordt insisted his secret formula of cleaning weapons was the best, but it was some damn god awful smelling crap that he laid his rifles in. They came out pretty good, but damn that shit smelled real bad. We emphasized to the recruits that the effort they and placed on the inspections was the same effort they should put on all inspections in the Corps. "If you ladies don't do it now with us on your ass you sure as hell won't do it later." You must start to discipline yourselves and do things on your own. Attention to detail as always was the key, we not only wanted them to pass and understand this concept but we of course wanted to outshine anyone else, passing or average was not good enough we needed to be "Out Fucking Standing."

The morning of final inspection found all three of us present once again. "Once you shower and shave and I mean shave everything but your damn eyebrows, you will report to Drill Instructor Sgt. Morse, then to me then you will go and put your socks and shoes on, and wait for further instructions. Is the Understood?" "Sir, Yes Sir!" The recruits would once again be in an assembly line, Sgt Morse had the ears, nose and fingernail detail, and I had the shaves, mouthwash and bug juice detail. The recruits would report to each one of us after showering and shaving. Sgt Morse would check to make sure they had cleaned their ears, their nose hair trimmed and fingernails short and cleaned. Once they left his station I would have them rinse out with mouthwash, check their shaves and than splash on some bug juice. Civilians call it aftershave. "What's the matter with you? I bet you have more hair growing out your nose than out your ass!, Dumbo Ears, damn it! You have enough shit in your ears to plant and feed the entire Marine Corps. Your Call that a shave? Get your ass back in and do it again, Peach Fuss Lips! What I didn't tell you to spit out the mouthwash, swallow that Listerine, makes your breath smell nice and fresh. Wow, Pizza Face look at you, your face is all cleared up, didn't I tell you that the Listerine would work! Your Mommy won't recognize you without all those zits. Put on some of my bug juice, you earned it, No! a big dose, I want you to smell better than a French WhoreHouse. Mouse come here, you too deserve a extra dose of my bug juice, get rid of that damn Mouse odor!" This assembly line was not unique to our herd, it was being played out in each squad bay of the barracks. "Now, Ladies put your skivvy shirts, then your shirts on, then your garters." Yeah, I said garters, we had taken elastic and sewed them to garter holders, you know like the women wear to keep their stocking up. They attached them to the bottom of their shirts, then to their socks, the shirt was then tight and fitted to the body and not a wrinkle could be seen. Some day somebody would market this shit and make a fortune. Now the recruits were instructed to put their trousers on, no not sitting down, they would step on top of their footlockers and then put them on. This way the trousers don't wrinkle. Then their belts and buckles, once snapped into place with the end of the buckle aligned with the zipper and shirt seam, they than took their handkerchief and wiped their brass so no fingermarks could be seen. Attention to detail! With each phase of the dressing directed by us, Yeah, the recruits even dressed by the numbers, this was a ritual they learned and would do over and over again once they left us. " Well girls, are we ready?" "Sir, Yes Sir!" "I can't hear you, I said are we ready?" "Sir, Yes Sir!" Final Inspection unlike the recruit's first inspection would be conducted by our Battalion Commander, the LtCol and of course accompanied by the SgtMaj. Our company Commander would also make up the rest of the Battalion Commander's entourage. The Battalion Commander would normally just do a quick walk through of the Series, followed by the detail inspectors, Officers from the rest his Battalion. We D.I.'s take notes, for the detailed inspector's as they went up and down the ranks of our recruits. The recruits would execute the manual of Inspection Arms with their weapons, and answer any questions asked while their weapon and uniforms were inspected. The recruits expected this to be like their first inspection with all hell breaking loose, we of course told them that this was the Grand Daddy of all Inspections. They knew if they screwed up. We might just shit can them on the spot. The primary difference from this inspection and their first inspection was not the inspectors. It was the recruits. They were ready for everything and anything, answering questions with confidence, almost to the point of mocking the inspectors. Ask me anything, they seemed to say, because I'm ready! Sure they screwed up a few, that was to be expected and those that did would be corrected. Most of the discrepancies were limited to a few Irish pennants and some botched answers, but this was the exception rather than the rule. If this had not been the case the Battalion Commander would probably fire our asses, and the SgtMaj administer a few quick chokes of his own.

"Well you bunch of Killers, you have exactly ten minutes to get out of your Inspection Uniform and then we practice for tomorrow's graduation." "Aye Aye Sir!" We would practice the sequence of events that would finally lead to the Command of Dismissed by the Plt. Cmdrs. Upon receiving this command the privates would join any family members that might have come to see them graduate. They would have four hours of base liberty. Meaning they could go anywhere on the Depot, the first time they had been given any such freedom in thirteen weeks. After the four hours they would report back to their barracks for one last night on MCRD San Diego. Buses would take them to Camp Pendleton and they would start their basic infantry training. After that they would be allowed to go home on ten days leave. Once their leave was completed, most would probably go to Advance Infantry Training, others would go on to whatever schools through out the Corps to learn the various skills of their Military Occupational Specialty (MOS).

Because we would start a new training syllabus with the next herd, this would be the last platoon to only get base liberty. The next platoon would be allowed to go home for ten days leave before their schooling. We would be taking them through their basic infantry training, adding two more weeks to Boot Camp. That damn Perez had been right! It made sense to do it this way, Hell we were already at Pendleton anyway for the rifle range and it gave us another two weeks to make sure they had their shit together.

The day before graduation was finally over. We had turned our weapons back into the Armory. All the final events done. Tonight would be another night where all of us would be present. At least until Taps (Lights Out), this was only fitting, we three had picked these turds up and it was only fitting that their last night as recruits, that the three of us stay on duty, at least until Taps. "House Mouse!" "Sir House Mouse!" "Get the classroom ready you little shit!" "Aye Aye Sir!" The Boss, Morse and myself entered the Squad Bay. Platoon Attention was sounded, the footlockers were in order and my Salems were placed correctly, upper right corner so I could read the label, now as the Mouse had anticipated correctly were three cups of coffee instead of just one. The Mouse had his shit together, and this classroom session was being carried out in each squad bay of the series. We had finally received the roster of MOS's for each of our recruits. Now we would inform them of what the Corps had in store for them for the rest of their enlistment. "Men! Be seated." "There was a slight hesitation from the platoon for the first time since we picked them up from the yellow footprints." "That's right, you shitheads, I said Men, now sit the fuck down!", yells the Boss. "Aye Aye Sir!" Instantly they were seated, eyes gleaming, shit the Plt Cmdr must be drunk or something he called us Men. "Thirteen weeks ago we met your sorry asses on the yellow footprints. Tomorrow you will graduate, tonight Drill Instructors Sgt. Hernandez and Sgt. Morse will call out your name and tell you what you will be doing in the Marine Corps and where you will be going for your training. It's almost over, but until you get your scummy bodies on the buses for Camp Pendleton your asses or still ours, Understood!" "Sir, Yes Sir!" "I can't hear you!" "Sir, Yes Sir!" "Before we start with the names and MOS's, you all know that we have covered a helluva a lot of material and it wasn't always easy, nor was it meant to be. You have done things in the last thirteen weeks that you never thought you were capable of doing, tomorrow you become part of a brotherhood in the most elite military force in the world. What you do with the rest of your days in the Corps is up to you. We have screamed and pushed you to do things instantly and taught you the way of a basic Marine. You won't have crazy people screaming at you to do your job, and that's what I mean it is your job. You must continue to be disciplined and form a self-discipline so that you are your own D.I. We have taught you and you have also learned through formal class instruction the proud history of our Corps. A History made by men just like yourselves, You must always remember that a Marine never ever leaves another Marine, you must set goals, and I don't care if it is in the Corps or in Civilian life. Set them and then Go For It! You, after tomorrow, will be a special breed of cat, we have never been first to leave a battlefield and its up to you to make sure that legacy does not change. In the heat of battle, if you look left or right it will be your fellow Marine that is by your side, no one else but them and your God and neither will forsake you. Sure we have yelled, screamed and belittled you, in combat our country expects you to win, no room for crying or getting a case of the "I cant's." Further, in combat we are warriors, nothing less than animals, but always, always in any environment that is not combat, we are gentlemen. We respect others and ourselves, the Corps expects this and so does the civilian population. Tomorrow I best not hear you shitheads slip up with fuck this or that, I had better hear nothing but Yes Sir's or Yes Ma'am's. Is that Understood?" "Sir, Yes Sir!" "Let's find out what you people will be doing for my beloved Marine Corps.

We called out the names of each recruit, informing him of his job with our own embellishments as to the Corps choice of what recruit for what job. "Pizza Face, No, you will be a fucking truck driver, Lard Ass, I can't believe it! You are being assigned to Administration! Dumbo Ears, you got to be shitting me, you are going to Public Affairs, they must have thought those damn ears could be a fucking radio antenna. Secretary! You who does not know the Latin name for ragweed is going into intelligence, how you got that shit is beyond my comprehension. Guide, you are going to be a cook! Mouse you little shit you will be a 0300 a true to life fucking infantryman, a grunt! The Mouse was not the first to get the O300 MOS. The recruits had been sucking in their breath every time we let any other recruit know they had the MOS of a Grunt. Damn you turds! The 0300 MOS is the Corps! Remember, I don't give a rat's ass if you are a cook, truck driver, admin or even fucking public affairs, every Marine is a basic Rifle/Infantryman. You never know when you have to put down your pencil, stop your truck or quick your baking and take up a rifle and go on patrol or protect your position. That's why we all fire our weapons and go through basic infantry training. The Corps always has been and will always be Infantry! History has shown that the only way to ensure that the enemy had been defeated is for some guy on the ground to take a position and hold it. To close with and defeat the enemy! Ladies, that means a Marine and his rifle, and that is an unbeatable combination. Right!" "Sir, Yes Sir!" "Ah Roo Ah!"

"How many of you shitheads have not been choked?" A few of the recruits raised their hands, "Damn I can't believe you raised your hands, bunch of dumb shits! Well, we sure don't want anyone to feel left out, so we will just have to do a mass choke. So, I want the whole platoon to put their right hand out, now reach up and choke yourselves. Do It!" "Aye Aye Sir!" " Stop!" the entire platoon was grasping for air as they had choked themselves almost to the point of passing out, but they were all smiling. Shaking our heads the Boss voiced our collective opinion, "You sure are a bunch of dumb turds, choking yourselves, but we have to admit, you are our turds at least until tomorrow. Ain't the fucking right Killer's!" "Sir, Yes Sir!" "Come on, let me hear it like you have a set!" "Sir, Yes Sir!" " Prepare for hygiene inspection, we will shower and shave in the morning so you will all smell nice for your Mommies and Daddy's and maybe your girlfriends."

"Lights Out!" "Sir, Lights Out, Aye Aye Sir!" "Tonight ladies as the Plt Cmdr and Drill Instructor Sgt. Morse depart the area. I would like to hear starting very softly and then towards the end, and at which point you had better be loud enough so those scummy civilians in San Diego hear you, sing my favorite song of the Marines Hymn. Can You Do It!" "Sir, Yes Sir!" "Do it! Yes, music to my ears, sing it out you bunch of Killers, You Devil Dogs, Louder! Good Night !" "Sir, Good Night Sir!"

I knew the recruits were not all asleep. As I walked from one end of the squad bay to the other. In the darkness, all was quiet, all you could hear was the sound of my heels as they struck the deck, I walked the entire length of the bay, passing by each rack, knowing that the privates were wondering what the Hell I might have up my sleeve. Could it be one last pit call, some late night ritual they were not aware of? Maybe I would wake their asses up and give them facing movements in the rack, just to screw with them? What they did not know is that I did this with every platoon and found out from other Hats that they also had some type of ritual they did with each one of their herds, the night before graduation. All of our thoughts seem to be the same, regardless of the ritual performed. Would we be graduating only those worthy of the title Marine, and of those that graduated, how many would survive the challenges we knew the Corps would give them. Whether it be in the Nam or any other conflict we might have to face. As I passed by each rack I mentally gave that recruit a thumbs up, this one would do well or on some occasions, said a little prayer because of some instinctive doubt I might have about a certain individual.

We had taught them the best we knew how, they all seemed so very young, but they had met the challenge and tomorrow they would graduate and the rest was up to them.

Graduation day had finally arrived, the recruits had showered and shaved and dressed in their tropical uniforms. They did not need to be dressed by the numbers, they knew the proper sequence, socks and shoes first, then your shirt, garters and then trousers. They marched smartly and proudly to the Depots Theater, every step taken to our cadence, eighty feet striking the deck at the same time, sounding as if one giant foot hit each time we called out "Left, Right, Left."

They entered the theater and were commanded, "Ready Seat!" The entire series hit their seats as one person. Those that were lucky had family members already seated, trying to see their son or boyfriend in the mass of young men now seated. The ceremony was a lot of Hoop-La about how the training went, individual awards were given out. You know, the recruit who fired highest on the range, for each platoon and the series, some recruits were even promoted to Private First Class (E-2). These were the recruits that had shown leadership, and had been able to assume responsibility, recruits like the Squad Leaders, Guide, Secretary and Yes, the House Mouse. All of this was given by the Battalion Commander, with the help of the Battalion Sgt. Maj. The Old Man had been introduced by the Company Commander, who in turn introduced the L.T. and he then introduced us. More words on how hard the training had been and how proud the parents should be of their sons. The Battalion Commander then shouts "MARINES, OF LIMA COMPANY, ON YOUR FEET!" Then again as one person, the entire series is on their feet, now addressing the series and for the benefit of the civilian on-lookers. "Marines, I know this is the first time you have been called that, you may have been called many other things, but never Marine. You have earned that title and the respect that the name has earned because of those Marines that have gone before you. Make sure that you continue the loyalty, courage, devotion to duty, love for your country that many a Marine has lost his life to defend. Plt Cmdrs form your platoons in front of the theater for the final phase of graduation." The series now marches out of the theater and forms in a series formation, in front of the theater, marching to the music played by the Depots Marching Band, playing the Marines Hymn. Our Company Commander is in position and faces the Series Officer, He commands our L.T. to take charge of his men. Salutes are exchanged and the L.T. does a perfect about face and now faces the Plt. Cmdr's and the Series. "Platoon Commanders take charge of your platoon and dismiss them!" They salute the L.T. and each Platoon Commander in platoon sequence will give them the command of Dismissed. The Boss, faces our herd and gives the command of "Platoon 3009 Dismissed!" A thunderous "Aye Aye Sir" is screamed by each new Marine, they then do an about face and its over, they are now Marines.

Its a pretty sight, the privates will now have their four hours of base liberty, most will go to the Exchange (Store) and chow down on burgers and fries, poggie bait, all those items they had not touched in thirteen weeks. Those with loved ones at the graduation, will show them around the Depot, taking them to their barracks, obstacle course, bayonet training area and probably even show them the pits. They will tell them all kinds of bullshit. About how hard we had been on them, how we made them run when they were tired, eat chow they didn't like, yelled and screamed at them. Knowing that those listening. Who had never been through the training, would look at them in awe, wondering how they survived. They had to say their good-byes and be back at the barracks by 1700 (5pm). That would give them time to get their gear together go to chow and be ready for the morning bus ride to Camp Pendleton and their basic Infantry Training.

It was all over for them, we of course would pick-up another herd within two days. Meet them on the yellow footprints and start the cycle all over again. I know the Battalion Commander had called them Marines and even with all the shit we had given them for the last thirteen weeks, I could never be sure that the name Marine really did mean anything to them. I saw the transformation and even their own parents could not believe the change from the boy that had left them into the young man that now greeted them. We had preached our Marine History, our traditions, our motto of Semper Fidelis (Always faithful). Even so, I always had doubts with every herd that we graduated, did it really mean what it was suppose to mean. You know, deep down inside where it really counts. Were they Marines because they made it through Boot Camp and had the name or were they **MARINES,** did we get through to them and instill that pride, self-discipline and loyalty.

Always, Always, my doubts were put to rest, some turd would be the one to set me straight. This time it happen to be the House Mouse. That little shit of ours that made the duty hut livable. "Sir House Mouse requests permission to speak to the Drill Instructor!" "What do you want *MARINE?*" At the name *MARINE*, his eyes bugged out, his chest got as big as it could possibly get without exploding, his jaws locked, and then he got that **fucking gleam of pride in his eyes that said it all.**

I knew from that gleam that the transformation was complete and the **Mystique** would continue to *live on and on.*

EPILOGUE

The kinship that is the Corps has not faded among the Marine's in this book. Those Marine's in our Series continue to be good friends. We have shared many memories and have told many stories and to a man whish we could do it all over again. I thought it would be interesting for the readers to know what happened to some of the Marines in our Series.

The L.T. continued in the Corps retiring at the rank of Full Colonel (0-6) after Commanding a Marine Battalion and Regiment. Not bad, having been throw out of the D.I.'s Head!

The Series Gunn's., who influenced so many of us Hat's, retired as a 1stSgt (E-8).

Ssgt Yordt, remains a close friend and retired as a MGySgt (E-9)

Ssgt Mimiaga retired as a Major (0-4), Sgt. Perez (Sammy), retired as a SgtMaj (E-9). Sgt. Morse retired as a MgySgt (E-9), Sgt. Tagleri (GodFather to my daughter) retired as a Major (0-4) and the Boss Ssgt Navarre retired as a Chief Warrant Officer (CWO-4), Both the Boss and Tag also remain close friends. **Semper Fi!**